Results and Performance of the
World Bank Group 2015

AN INDEPENDENT EVALUATION

WORLD BANK GROUP
World Bank • IFC • MIGA

Careful observation and analysis of program data and the many issues impacting program efficacy reveal what works as well as what could work better. The knowledge gleaned is valuable to all who strive to ensure that World Bank goals are met and surpassed.

contents

Appendixes

The appendixes to this report are available at
https://ieg.worldbankgroup.org/evaluations/results-and-performance-2015

Boxes

Figures

Tables

Evaluation Managers   Caroline Heider, *Director-General, Evaluation*

Nicholas York, *Director, IEGHE*

Marie Gaarder, *Manager, IEGHC*

Midori Makino and Sidney Edelmann, *Task Managers, IEGSP*

abbreviations

CY	calendar year (for IFC)
DOTS	Development Outcome Tracking System
DPF	development policy financing
FY	fiscal year (for World Bank)
FCS	fragile and conflict-affected situation
GP	Global Practice
IBRD	International Bank for Reconstruction and Development
ICR	Implementation Completion and Results
ICRR	Implementation Completion and Results Review
IDA	International Development Association
IEG	Independent Evaluation Group
IFC	International Finance Corporation
IPF	investment project financing
ISR	Implementation Status and Results
M&E	monitoring and evaluation
MAR	Management Action Record
MIGA	Multilateral Investment Guarantee Agency
MS	moderately satisfactory (rating)
MU	moderately unsatisfactory (rating)
PDO	project development objective
RAP	Results and Performance
SME	small and medium enterprise

acknowledgments

This report was prepared by a team led by Midori Makino and Sid Edelmann. The analyses were carried out under the guidance of Nick York (Director) and Marie Gaarder (Manager), as well as the direction of Caroline Heider (Director-General, Evaluation). Elena Bardasi coordinated the analyses on gender, and Brenda Barbour coordinated the analyses related to the Management Action Record. Claude Leroy-Themeze led the six Region Updates team. Kavita Mathur led the preparation of the three clusters of Global Practices updates as well as data analysis.

The core team consisted of Joy Behrens, Gisela Garcia, Eduardo Fernandez Maldonado, and Yoshine Uchimura. Nadia Asgaraly, Francesco Bolognesi, Leonardo Bravo, Nathyeli Yethzi Acuna Castillo, Unurjargal Demberel, Hiroyuki Hatashima, Kelly Andrews Johnson, Yunsun Li, Katia Ondina Diaz Morejon, Thao Nguyen, Zukhra Shaabdullaeva, and Fang Xu provided additional data analysis support.

The Region Updates team consisted of Surajit Goswami, Chukwuma Obidegwu, Luis Alvaro Sanchez, Anthony Martin Tyrrell, and Clay Wescott. Fernando Manibog prepared notes on three clusters of Global Practices with inputs from IEG thematic teams. An Influence Analysis note of IEG Evaluations and the Management Action Record (MAR) process was prepared by Soniya Carvalho and Anis Dani.

Peer reviewers were Aart Kraay (Senior Adviser, DECMG), Marco Segone (Director, Evaluation Office, United Nations Entity for Gender Equality and the Empowerment of Women), and Rakesh Nangia (Director of the Operations Evaluation Department of the African Development Bank).

Romayne Pereira provided administrative support to the team, and William Hurlbut and Anthony Martin Tyrrell provided editorial support to the team.

overview

THE INDEPENDENT EVALUATION GROUP'S (IEG) *Results and Performance of the World Bank Group* (RAP) is a comprehensive assessment of World Bank Group performance, drawing on recent IEG evaluations. The report also examines how effectively the World Bank Group addressed current and emerging development challenges. This year's RAP focuses on gender integration in World Bank Group operations, building on previous examinations of World Bank Group approaches to risk management (RAP 2013) and the Millennium Development Goals (RAP 2014). This report also reviews how effectively the World Bank Group's portfolio and country programs deliver results, and its system for monitoring the implementation of IEG's recommendations.

"No country, community, or economy can achieve its potential or meet the challenges of the 21st century without the full and equal participation of women and men, girls and boys." This statement from the World Bank Group website's topic page on gender states the essential importance of gender for development. In line with that view, the World Bank Group made considerable progress in addressing gender issues during the past 15 years. Gender has been a prominent corporate objective since the first World Bank Group strategy, introduced in 2001. This year, a new World Bank Group gender strategy has been launched—the first joint World Bank–International Finance Corporation (IFC) strategy to focus on gender. It is an important step toward sharpening the corporate focus on gender and improving the approach to gender mainstreaming.

This report describes how mechanisms for integrating gender in projects and country strategies are working, and to what extent they provide meaningful information about progress and results on gender. The analysis aims to inform World Bank Group efforts to strengthen the approach to documenting, assessing, and evaluating results as part of the new strategy rollout.

Corporate commitments have helped broaden policy and strategy attention to gender, which increased gender uptake. However, the quality of gender integration was uneven. Corporate commitments on gender were agreed, and reflected in, the results framework of the 16th Replenishment of the International Development Association (IDA16) and IDA17, and in the World Bank Group Corporate Scorecard. The commitments were monitored through the introduction of gender flags, mandatory disaggregation of project beneficiaries, and inclusion of gender indicators in IFC's Development Outcome Tracking System. The gender mainstreaming strategy was successful in increasing gender uptake (the number and percentage of operations and country strategies that addressed gender issues at entry). This uptake is more notable in recent years.

At the same time, progress in including gender integration at entry (the increase in the rate of projects defined as "gender-informed") was not matched by similar attention to quality and depth of gender integration. Current guidelines refer to integrating gender when relevant, but they do not define relevance, resulting in variable practice. The portfolio review revealed that projects—and especially country strategies—do not clearly identify gender relevance, and therefore struggle to clearly articulate an explicit results chain and select appropriate indicators for measuring results.

Country strategies are required to integrate gender by corporate commitments, and they generally do this. Most country strategies identify gender as a cross-cutting theme, delegating the explanation of the rationale and results chain to individual projects within the country portfolio. This effectively dilutes the strategy focus on the country gender priorities that need to be addressed.

The monitoring and evaluation (M&E) frameworks of operations and country strategies do not adequately measure and report on gender results. Tracking, reporting, and assessing gender results have become a higher organizational priority in the recent period, reflected in the corporate commitment to tracking female beneficiaries. An increasing number of projects report this indicator; several added it during implementation. When indicators were integrated at an early stage and were grounded in concrete actions and components, reporting on the indicators was substantial. This was true for both projects and country strategies—reporting on the indicators was typically sound when gender actions were identified and were supported by a relevant background diagnostic, and when indicators were integrated into Country Assistance Strategy programs. Qualitative reporting of indicators is more frequent than quantitative reporting, but both have serious limitations, including poorly reported indicators, vague qualitative statements, incoherent reporting, and not reporting indicators at all.

However, weaknesses in M&E frameworks prevent meaningful tracking and assessment of projects' and country strategies' gender results. Nearly all country strategies reviewed incorporated gender in at least some dimension, but only a few had internally consistent background analysis, actions, and indicators and corresponding results measured and reported. At the project level, development outcome indicators reflecting gender are rare, and many person-level indicators are still not sex-disaggregated, even when meaningful disaggregation was technically feasible. Defining and counting female beneficiaries, though increasingly done, requires more than counting recipients or residents of the project area, and involves measuring both the direct and broader distributional impacts. For both country strategies and projects, indicators used are often inadequate to capture gender results because they are frequently narrow in scope and tend to measure outputs rather than outcomes.

The new World Bank Group gender strategy offers an opportunity to improve tracking and reporting of gender results. The introduction of the first World Bank Group gender strategy in fiscal year 2016 (FY16) is an opportunity to ensure that the mechanisms established to support gender integration in country strategies and projects are fine-tuned to generate and produce meaningful information and reporting. IEG's analysis shows this can be achieved by moving away from a purely mechanical observance of corporate mandates and a box-ticking culture to embrace a more consistent, robust approach that involves identifying priorities, articulating a results chain, selecting meaningful indicators, following up coherently, and monitoring and reporting the results achieved.

The performance of Bank lending, IFC Advisory Services, and Multilateral Investment Guarantee Agency (MIGA) guarantees remains stable, but the performance of IFC investments continues to decline. World Bank Group commitments peaked in FY10 after the global financial crisis, but lending tapered off through 2013. Commitments are now rising once again and have increased for two consecutive years. Commitments reached $60 billion in FY15. Weighted by commitment size, the performance of World Bank projects for the period FY12–14 exceeded FY17 corporate targets; measured by number (unweighted percentage), performance held steady, but was below the FY17 corporate target. The performance of Bank projects in East Asia and Pacific resisted the overall trend, declining in FY12–14 to a performance rating just above the Middle East and North Africa Region. Among the Global Practices, performance was particularly strong in Social Protection and Labor, and in Agriculture.

IFC advisory and MIGA guarantee products continued to perform well, but IFC investment lending continued the downward trend first reported in 2013. Falling equity success, influenced by ongoing fallout from the financial crisis and global economic slowdown, affected investment success. Investment project performance improved in IDA and blend countries, but continued to dip significantly otherwise, reflecting poor investment outcomes and work quality, particularly in the manufacturing and services industry group, and in the Europe and Central Asia and East Asia and Pacific Regions.

Midcourse corrections matter more than project size for successful performance in World Bank projects; for IFC projects, size matters for real sector projects, but less than do other risk factors. Using statistical analysis, IEG found that initial commitment size is not a key element of success for World Bank investment lending projects, but the change in project size during the project cycle is a significant correlate of a project outcome rating. Additional financing is typically introduced for what are deemed well-performing projects, which increases their size, but does not cause their success. Performance can improve by paying more attention to certain factors at entry, such as risk assessment, relative design complexity, and clear objectives. Currently, quality at entry is not systematically rated at the beginning of the project.

The analysis also found that higher outcome ratings were associated with projects in countries with higher Country Policy and Institutional Assessment ratings, when controlling for country- and project-specific characteristics, Global Practice, and region. Lower project outcome ratings were associated with task manager turnover, higher supervision cost, and whether the project was ever labeled a problem project. Related analysis suggests that early and candid assessment of project implementation performance is important because lack of corrective actions or untimely restructuring were the key reasons for poor project outcomes. Projects in countries with greater gender equality, more effective government functions, or more stable rule of law were also associated with higher outcome ratings.

For IFC projects, IEG found that project size was a significant correlate of development results for real sector projects, but not for banking projects. However, for real sector projects, the association of commitment size with development success diminished as other risk factors were added to the model. For these projects, external project risks (such as management quality, market conditions, investment climate, and internal controllable risk factors in IFC's work quality) are more significantly correlated with development outcomes.

Using the identified factors associated with development outcomes, analysis to predict the performance of IFC projects revealed that recently committed IFC projects are likely to perform worse than recently evaluated projects, despite a larger concentration of recent IFC commitments in less risky countries.

Outcomes of country programs for International Bank for Reconstruction and Development (IBRD) and IDA have improved during the past three years and remained stable in fragile and conflict-affected situations, with a higher success rate than for the World Bank Group average. Improvement is led mostly by the Europe and Central Asia and Latin America and the Caribbean Regions. The performance of the World Bank Group in designing and implementing country programs deteriorated slightly overall, especially in Latin America and the Caribbean. It improved in all other regions including Africa, or remained stable.

The Management Action Record (MAR) process was successful in creating a formal, transparent, and well-understood structure within the organization for reporting about progress made to address recommendations in IEG evaluations. IEG evaluations make recommendations to improve the development effectiveness of the World Bank Group. IEG and management then monitor the implementation of actions associated with those recommendations to promote accountability and generate knowledge about where improvements are and are not made. The World Bank Group's Boards of Executive Directors can use the MAR as a tool to hold World Bank Group management accountable for actions to which it committed.

Between FY12 and FY14, IEG produced 25 corporate, sector, and thematic evaluations, resulting in 170 recommendations being tracked using the MAR. This year, as in previous years, IEG found that implementation of those recommendations improves over time. IEG rates implementation of just over 80 percent of the recommendations substantial or better by year four.

However, M&E recommendations have eluded meaningful response. Implementation progress is even across all major recommendations categories except for M&E quality. For M&E, World Bank Group management generally agreed with IEG's recommendations, but implementation was difficult because of issues with data collection, assessment methodologies, and the time required for outcomes to materialize. Management acknowledged these difficulties and rated implementation substantial for only half of M&E-related recommendations in the fourth year of implementation, which is well below average.

The MAR could be an even more effective tool if it were less formalistic and more purpose driven, and if active, deliberative, and ongoing dialogue were integrated throughout the process.

The MAR is a useful accountability tool, but the process requires further reform to make it an effective tool for learning. Interviews with selected IEG and World Bank Group managers and staff involved with the six evaluations entering their fourth year of follow-up revealed that the evaluations themselves have more influence than the recommendations alone. Many managers and staff interviewed considered the MAR follow-up to be a static, bureaucratic accounting exercise that resulted in little deep reflection on progress. Recommendations are tracked even when they may have lost their relevance as the operational environment and strategic priorities evolved.

The review identified three major factors that contributed to an evaluation's influence. Timely evaluations that generated findings and recommendations aligned with ongoing strategic priorities and operational programs tended to have relatively strong adoption of recommendations. World Bank Group managers and staff also said they were more likely to take an evaluation and its recommendations seriously if they considered its analysis to be of high quality and the evaluation team technically credible. Management also cited the value of early and frequent engagement with evaluation teams as a factor in their receptiveness to findings and recommendations.

Still, it was also noted that for some evaluations that address difficult or cross-cutting issues with unclear ownership, early engagement with the right stakeholders may not be achieved. Such evaluations may be among the most influential in the longer run, but the influence may take a longer time, and avenues of influence other than what the MAR can offer may be required. A statement in the Independent Panel's report to the Committee on Development Effectiveness stressed the importance of IEG's strategic engagement and a close but uncompromised relationship with management and staff.

Further reforms of the MAR process should seek to encourage earlier and deeper engagement between evaluators, management, and topical stakeholders.

management comments

WORLD BANK GROUP MANAGEMENT welcomes the report of the Independent Evaluation Group (IEG), *Results and Performance of the World Bank Group 2015,* and the opportunity to respond with comments. The report brings out many salient issues and provides useful analysis and insights on three key topics: (a) the integration of gender into Bank Group operations and country strategies; (b) results and performance of recent Bank Group operations; and (c) the Management Action Record (MAR).

Bank Group management welcomes IEG's recognition of recent positive trends as well as of challenges in the results and performance of Bank Group operations. These include (a) the good progress in gender mainstreaming in recent years, in particular the increased gender uptake in operations and country strategies; (b) the good performance of Bank lending, International Finance Corporation (IFC) Advisory Services, and Multilateral Investment Guarantee Agency (MIGA) guarantees; and (c) the overall improvement in the performance of Bank Group country programs.

World Bank Management Comments

Gender Integration

The report reflects on the Bank Group's experience in gender mainstreaming and draws some lessons that also informed the new Bank Group Gender Strategy published in December 2015. The new Bank Group Gender Strategy emphasizes the importance of defining specific gender gaps on which to focus in Country Partnership Frameworks, approaches to address and track such gaps in the analytical and operational portfolio, and clear results chains on gender equality at the project and strategy level. It also highlights the critical role of country ownership, because achievements on closing gender gaps will only be sustained if they are integrated in countries' own development agenda and institutions.

Gender mainstreaming to gender integration. Management fully recognizes the need to strengthen the link between diagnostics and relevant interventions and outcomes at the country strategy and project levels. Much progress has been made since the 2001 Gender Strategy. The latest Bank Group Gender Strategy has greatly benefited from lessons learned over the past 15 years through the implementation of Country Gender Assessments and country and Regional Gender Action Plans, as well as from a wealth of analytical and evaluative work, notably the 2010 IEG evaluation of the implementation of the 2001 strategy and the 2012 World Development Report on gender.

The introduction of the three-dimension gender flags at the project and country levels in FY13 successfully raised the uptake of gender issues in country strategies and projects. Building on this success, the new Bank Group Gender Strategy aims to raise the bar by strengthening the links between country gender diagnostics and the identification of relevant interventions, and by enhancing the quality and relevance of monitoring and evaluation (M&E) frameworks for improved reporting of gender-related results. Management appreciates the analysis and examples of indicators in projects and country strategies (in the text and Box 1.3) and the focus on outcomes, which enhance learning and provide a useful reference point as we implement the Bank Group Gender Strategy. Revised guidelines for the inclusion of gender equality outcomes in the Systematic Country Diagnostic and Country Partnership Framework documents are under development and will be available by the end of FY16.

Global Practices and IFC departments are developing follow-up notes for how they will implement the Bank Group Gender Strategy. These plans will discuss the gender gaps they can help close, highlight good practices and approaches in operational programs, and identify areas for which more piloting and research are needed. IFC industry departments and five Global Practice follow-up notes are already under development, and the remainder will follow in FY17.

More systematic diagnostics and monitoring. Management plans to address the gaps identified in the report through a more systematic approach, including (a) enhanced country diagnostics that not only identify specific gender gaps but also probe into the underlying causes and constraints for those gaps; (b) support for more and better sex-disaggregated data at the country and global levels; and (c) a new monitoring system for projects using an enhanced three-dimension gender tag and monitoring indicators throughout the project cycle.

As the 2015 strategy explained, the gender tag has been revised, with sharper definitions and questions that better link project-relevant gender gaps and those identified through the country engagement framework. The new gender tag has already been introduced for all investment project financing (IPF) operations. Progress will be monitored at project entry and throughout implementation and completion, including through a new outcome rating, of how well the activity closed gender gaps, in the Implementation Completion and Results (ICR). Implementation of the new monitoring system has already commenced: the trial phase for the new gender tag system is under way, and working groups have been formed for the development of revised rating criteria, relevant guidelines, and so forth. Following the successful completion of the trial phase, gradual rollout is expected to start in FY17, with the first phase targeting Bank IPF operations.

The Bank Group Gender Strategy also takes on the challenges highlighted in the report, both in the availability of relevant data and the necessary skills to use these data and improve the quality of gender analysis at the country level and in operations.

Methodology for the country strategy and project reviews. The *a posteriori* application of the gender flag to the analysis of country strategies ignores the fact that the scorecard assessed country strategies presented to the Board in FY15, while the review considers country strategies that closed between FY12 and FY14, that is, before the analysis of the three dimensions became part of International Development Association (IDA) monitoring. Similarly, the *a posteriori* application of the gender flag to the analysis of projects should be tempered because many sample projects that were closed between FY12 and FY14 were designed and implemented before the flag system was put in place.

Recent Results and Performance of World Bank Operations

Management appreciates the comprehensive presentation of project outcomes information with different levels of disaggregation—by project counts versus commitment amount, IPF versus development policy financing, International Bank for Reconstruction and Development (IBRD) versus IDA, by Region, and by Global Practice (GP). Such disaggregation enables a deeper analysis to pinpoint areas of weaker performance and enriches the discussion. The Regional and Practice Group updates attached to the report are a very useful tool to highlight each group's overall portfolio characteristics, as well as its trends, strengths, and challenges in performance. Management also appreciates the report's recognition of some of the concrete steps taken to address performance challenges.

Factors affecting project outcomes. Management also appreciates the report's detailed analysis on factors affecting project outcomes, which is a rich source of information and insights. Not surprisingly, quality at entry, quality of supervision, and M&E quality are among the top factors affecting project performance. Client capacity and commitment, project management, and experience and turnover of Bank task team leaders also play important roles. A deeper analysis to understand project-specific factors and context may be useful—for instance, the relationship between project restructuring and outcome ratings.

Project size. Management notes the finding that changes in commitments during implementation (through cancellation or additional financing) are significantly associated with outcome ratings, while the correlation with initial commitment size was not significant. Figure 2.11 also confirms this intuitive result since, as the report points out, additional financing (or cancellation) is often an effect of good (or poor) performance, not a cause.

Risk. The report underemphasizes the recent developments to strengthen the identification of risks and mitigation measures. Under the Systematic Operations Risk-rating Tool (SORT) framework, introduced in October 2014, risk is defined as it relates to the achievement of intended development outcomes and the risk of unintended impact of an operation or country engagement. The SORT is a simple tool designed to identify risk early on and throughout the project cycle, systematically track progress, and continuously assess its effect. This information can effectively contribute to improvements, not only in quality at entry, but also vis-à-vis the development results that the operations were designed to achieve.

Crisis response. Management appreciates the observation that the global food crisis projects supported by the Bank are seen to have "performed exceptionally well." On avian influenza, the Annex notes the positive experience and the Bank's "ability to use its convening power, to raise funds, to work with partners, and to rapidly prepare and supervise a global investment program." It also highlights how the Bank continues to support important global agendas even after the spotlight has moved on. For example, the Agriculture Global Practice has recently made concerted efforts to resuscitate the Global Food Crisis Response Trust Fund and will use the available funds to mount analytical support in response to the El Niño phenomenon, which affects several client countries.

Management Action Record (MAR)

It is encouraging to note the high rates of implementation of IEG recommendations after four years. A key remaining challenge is the recommendations on M&E: only two of the four recommendations showed substantial or better implementation progress by year four. The upcoming reform of the Implementation Completion and Results (ICR) report will present an important opportunity to strengthen guidance and tools for self-evaluation of projects. Management is also taking actions to step up staff training in M&E and results measurement.

Management is already working with IEG to strengthen the MAR process with earlier and more collaborative interactions between IEG evaluators and operations staff. The proposed dynamic engagement and dialogue to promote learning and adaptable implementation of recommendations is also welcomed by management. As a follow-up to the recommendations from the IEG External Review, management and IEG are planning to implement a few pilot processes to that effect.

IFC Management Comments

Management appreciates IEG's review and analyses detailed in the World Bank Group *Results and Performance 2015*. It commends IEG for highlighting gender as a featured evaluation topic this year, particularly given the new Bank Group Gender Strategy, and for providing candid insights from recent results based on IEG-validated self-evaluation systems and other studies. Management also appreciates IEG's undertaking an analysis of the influence of project size on investment success. The report overall is helpful in drawing attention to important areas for IFC to consider as it continuously seeks to improve operational performance.

Development Results. With respect to IFC's investment services, management acknowledges that the share of positively rated projects in the evaluated sample for CY12–14 declined to 58 percent on an unweighted basis, or 69 percent weighted by commitment size, from 73 percent for CY08–10. In this regard, management agrees with the report that the development performance of IFC investments is closely linked to the financial success of those investments and that it was significantly impacted by the global economic and financial crisis throughout the period of CY07–14, as well as region-specific effects in Europe and the Middle East. Global economic conditions affected the equity portfolio in particular, which has become a larger share of IFC's business over the review period. With respect to IFC's **equity investments, however, management wishes to note that they have consistently outperformed against relevant global emerging-market benchmarks, and IFC manages equity investments with a long-term approach.** Furthermore, widespread economic volatility, accompanied by currency depreciation and low commodity prices, continued to affect both developed and developing countries.

The report also points to work quality as one of the key factors affecting IFC investment development outcomes. IFC management acknowledges the analysis, and views this as an important opportunity to identify potential improvements in work quality. Based on a further review of evaluated projects, it is difficult to discern a systematic pattern from the data. IFC therefore plans to undertake a further analysis jointly with IEG to examine the data in more granular detail to identify causality at the process, product, industry, or regional level. Following the analysis, actionable recommendations linked to more specific findings on where work quality can be improved will be identified. This work will be done in conjunction with the diagnostic exercise launched by IFC's Executive Vice President.

With respect to Advisory Services, management acknowledges IEG's recognition of the steady development effectiveness of IFC's Advisory Services in the report. The success rate in the most recent three-year rolling period (CY12–14) was 75 percent by self-rating, based on all the applicable advisory portfolio, compared to the 63 percent reflected in the report after IEG adjustments. Strong performance has been steady over the past five years and is expected to continue per CY15 preliminary data. This is consistent with a 91 percent client satisfaction rate reported through client surveys. Management is pleased with the stable success backed by strong work quality assessed by IEG, including over the period of reorganization of IFC's Advisory Services. One and a half years have passed since the reorganization took place; it would be useful for IEG to start reporting results against the current structure.

Methodology. Management is aware of methodological differences between IEG and IFC, particularly on evaluation of IFC's investment operations. The IFC team looks forward to resolving them with IEG. For instance, the more significant decline in the IEG system than that in the Development Outcome Tracking System (DOTS) is influenced by the fact that the former does not update project performance for the sample even if the financial performance of the underlying investments improves after the Expanded Project Supervision Report (XPSR) is validated by IEG. This is an important consideration, given the timeframe. The implementation period of the projects in the sample, conceived and approved by the Board in CY07–09, included the global financial crisis, Eurozone slowdown, and such geopolitical events as those in Eastern Europe and the Middle East. Because IFC held on to the evaluated investments after IEG validation, DOTS has captured net performance improvement for the entire active portfolio which may have taken place after conditions started to stabilize.

Signs of weakening development outcomes are also evident in the success rate generated by IFC's internal and portfolio-wide DOTS. The DOTS success rate stood at 66 percent for FY12–14, and the decline from 71 percent for FY08–10 was more modest. Management further acknowledges that IFC's preliminary self-rating for the same CY12–14 XPSR sample stood at 73 percent on a non-weighted basis. Management is pleased to learn that the difference in the success rate between IFC's review and IEG's has narrowed to 13 percentage points in CY13. Management encourages IEG to assess projects and IFC's work based on the information that was available to project teams at the time they engaged in the rated activities. Management understands that a detailed memo with full analysis of rating differences will be issued to IFC and looks forward to further discussions together with the above-mentioned joint analysis.

Another instance of differences is in respect to IFC's additionality framework established in 2007, and IEG's role and contribution framework embedded in the XPSRs. For instance, IFC considers "long-term partnership" and "provision of equity not available in the market" as important forms of additionality, while IEG does not recognize them as such. According to IFC's client survey, long-term partnership is the most cited reason why investment clients choose to work with IFC. In addition, the provision of equity not available in the market can be essential to the viability of an investment.

Gender Operationalization in IFC. Management appreciates IEG's undertaking a special thematic analysis regarding the Bank Group's gender integration and is pleased with the report's recognition of IFC's initiatives in integrating gender into its strategy and operations, with notable progress in recent years. As described, IFC has come a long way in its selective gender mainstreaming efforts since its first gender-dedicated projects in 2005. This now includes the launch of a gender flag, first in advisory projects and then in investments; the establishment of a Gender Secretariat, the Bank Group Gender Cross-Cutting Solutions Area (CCSA), and the recently endorsed Bank Group Gender Strategy (FY16–23); three new gender-focused advisory solutions (employment, insurance, and women business and leadership training); and the large Banking on Women portfolio. Management is proud of the achievements IFC has made in helping and promoting gender equality in the private sector and beyond. As IEG observed, IFC has been strategically focused in the way it operationalizes gender with clients. Implementation has contributed to closing gaps between men and women when it comes to access to jobs and assets, but management recognizes that even more can be done. With clients in targeted areas, IFC's approach has been to seek to support the projects' gender-related needs, which are typically implemented as specific activities rather than as defined objectives. Investments in the Banking on Women program, currently consisting of 32 projects, do have a clear-cut gender objective, along with DOTS targets and reporting, which are part of investment agreements. IFC's investment efforts also involve the appointment of women directors to the board seats of client companies, with a target of reaching 30 percent on IFC-seated boards. In FY14, IFC reached 28 percent of women as non-executive directors being nominated into its board seats. Going forward, IFC is looking to help more clients realize gender solutions to their business challenges.

Regarding IFC's Global Entrepreneurship Markets Initiative, implemented in Africa, management acknowledges the comments made in the report. These projects were the first cohort of micro, small, and medium enterprise projects in Africa with a gender component. The valuable lessons drawn from the challenges encountered during implementation of these projects have been addressed in subsequent project design—in particular, by focusing on phasing projects in a way that considers the client's internal capacity to implement. The Diamond Bank Burundi project was a stand-alone gender project, implemented by the same team that rolled out the early pilots, and similar lessons on client readiness have been effectively applied.

Regional Operations—Eastern Europe and Central Asia. The IEG evaluation states that the success rate of investments in Eastern Europe and Central Asia was on a downward trend, first reported in 2013. As noted above, the cohort of projects covered in the report was approved just before or during the global financial crisis, which affected the region the most severely because of its stronger linkages with the Eurozone, especially through the financial sector. The crisis significantly weakened the economic and financial performance of the projects in the cohort. Because IFC's clients do not operate in isolation from the rest of the economy, which was in recession as late as 2013, their performance could have been much worse without IFC's support, given the magnitude and persistence of the shocks that they were facing. Consequently, management believes that IFC investments in the Europe and Central Asia Region were among the most resilient, given the challenging environment. Regarding the overall assessment of economic challenges faced by the region related to the review period, management observed that low competitiveness driven by resource intensity (especially energy), poor financial intermediation, inadequate infrastructure, and a poor business-enabling environment also presented challenges to the region in addition to social inclusion, as spelled out in the Europe and Central Asia strategies for the past two years and reviewed by IEG.

In Kazakhstan, IFC responded vigorously with long-term lending targeted at small and medium enterprises (SMEs) to address issues in the financial sector during the 2008 crisis. In the real sector, IFC provided support with advisory services in many sectors of the economy. In parallel, IFC actively explored investment operations in an environment where suitable sponsors were scarce and the economy was dominated by state interests. Many projects did not materialize, mostly because of sponsor issues, high leverage, and low competitiveness. Since 2009, IFC has significantly increased investment activities in select sectors, consistent with its strategic priorities. Regarding better coordination on investment climate reform and SME development, management is pleased to share that the joint Trade and Competitiveness GP is enhancing coordination and that all current country strategies in the region are being delivered jointly and explicitly address SME issues.

MIGA Management Comments

Evidence base. Overall, MIGA finds that the Results and Performance (RAP) 2015 report provides a useful analysis of MIGA operations during the review period, based on FY09–14 project evaluations, with a Development Outcome (DO) success rate of 63 percent (35/56). RAP 2014 was based on FY08-13 project evaluations with a DO success rate of 70 percent (30/43). MIGA notes that while the longer (six-year) accumulation for DO success rate is sensible—given the small number of projects evaluated annually—the DO success rate variations in the yearly RAPs should be viewed in the context of the performance profile of project evaluations that enter and exit the portfolio in the RAP cycle.

Performance of MIGA guarantees. The report notes the performance of MIGA guarantee projects as stable with some weaknesses, particularly in the financial sector. MIGA notes that most of the weakly-performing financial sector projects were in the Europe and Central Asia Region and were supported in the wake of the global financial crisis, as MIGA's response to the crisis, in the broader context of the international financial institutions' initiatives. The magnitude and duration of the financial crisis have proved to be greater than expected and have been the main reason for the weak performance of financial sector projects. Many of the MIGA financial sector guarantee projects supported in the Europe and Central Asia Region were also supported by other international financial institutions (IFC, the European Bank for Reconstruction and Development, European Investment Bank), which seems to suggest that macro rather than micro factors were the key drivers of performance.

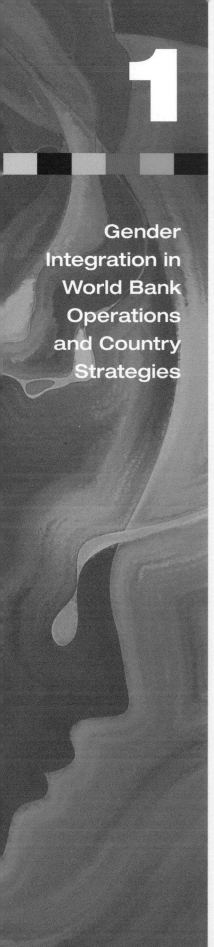

1

Gender Integration in World Bank Operations and Country Strategies

highlights

1 Strong corporate commitments were translated into guidelines and practices that were mostly process-oriented

2 The quality of gender integration in projects and country strategies—currently not measured in the World Bank Group monitoring system—can be improved

3 Projects and especially country strategies do not clearly identify gender relevance or articulate a results chain

4 Integrating gender as a cross-cutting theme in country strategies dilutes its focus

5 Weaknesses in monitoring and evaluation frameworks prevent meaningful tracking and assessment of projects' and country strategies' gender results. If the indicators are poor, results are not meaningful even if reported.

Introduction

THE WORLD BANK GROUP considerably advanced its gender agenda during the past 15 years. The first gender strategy (introduced in 2001 and supported by Bank policy OP/BP 4.20) recognized the importance of addressing gender to reduce poverty, and mandated that gender be mainstreamed in all country strategies and throughout the World Bank lending portfolio. At first, the consideration of gender issues was primarily limited to the human development field (education and health in particular). The Gender Action Plan (World Bank 2006) later expanded the focus to traditionally neglected sectors, such as infrastructure, agriculture, private sector development, and labor markets. The *World Development Report 2012: Gender Equality and Development* added further impetus to working toward gender equality. Finally, the World Bank Group restructuring in 2014 effectively made gender a top institutional priority by creating the Gender Cross-Cutting Solution Area (CCSA).

Progress in mainstreaming gender within the institution has not been linear. The 2010 IEG gender evaluation (IEG 2010) found that progress was stronger immediately after introduction of the gender strategy in 2001, but then weakened during 2005–08. The evaluation also identified some gaps in the implementation of OP/BP 4.20 (Box 1.1). Some of these gaps were addressed, as documented in the Management Action Record (MAR), by institutionalizing reporting mechanisms, intensifying efforts to produce sex-disaggregated data and impact evaluation evidence, and further strengthening results and accountability mechanisms. Corporate commitments on gender were agreed to and reflected in the results frameworks of International Development Association (IDA) Replenishments IDA16 and IDA17, and in the Corporate Scorecard. The Bank committed to disaggregating project beneficiaries by gender and instituted a gender flag at the project design stage in FY13.

The gender mainstreaming strategy was undoubtedly successful in increasing the gender uptake (the number and percentage of operations and country strategies that addressed gender issues at entry). This uptake is more notable in recent years. The annual reports (issued by the former Poverty Reduction and Economic Management Gender unit entitled *Update on the Implementation of the Gender Equality Agenda at the World Bank Group* (2012, 2013, 2014) documented a sharp increase in the share of World Bank Group lending operations that were gender informed in recent years—up to 95 percent of all approved lending operations in 2014.[1] Similarly, updates on the Corporate Scorecards reported that the institution's attention to gender resulted in 100 percent gender-informed country strategies.[2]

The 2001 World Bank gender strategy does not govern the International Finance Corporation (IFC), yet IFC promoted initiatives in recent years to integrate gender into its portfolio, such as the Gender Entrepreneurship Markets program, Banking on Women, the Women in Business Program, WINVest, and SheWorks. IFC is also one of the largest global investors in the microfinance sector, which

Box 1.1 | The 2010 IEG Gender Evaluation

IEG evaluated the effectiveness of the Bank's gender mainstreaming approach between FY02 and FY08 and concluded that the Bank made progress in gender integration, but implementation of the Bank's gender policy weakened in the latter half of the evaluation period. IEG also found that two gaps in the Bank's gender policy diminished the policy's relevance: the lack of a results framework in the 2001 Gender Strategy (World Bank 2002), and the replacement of a more generalized mainstreaming approach with a selective country-level approach. IEG made three recommendations:

- Foster greater clarity and better implementation of the Bank's gender policy by establishing a results framework and a plan for country-level diagnostics, among other things

- Establish clear management accountability for development and implementation of a monitoring system

- Strengthen the incentives for effective gender-related actions in country clients.

Management agreed with the recommendations and subsequently reported on actions taken to strengthen gender integration in World Bank work. Some of the activities reported in the Management Action Record (MAR) were the 2011 introduction of gender indicators in the Corporate Scorecard; institutionalization of reporting mechanisms; more systematic integration of gender in Country Assistance Strategies; and the introduction of Regional Gender Action Plans. At the country level, management identified lack of gender-relevant data as a key constraint, and reported on efforts to improve local statistical capacity through the Gender Equality Data and Statistics Working Group and the World Bank's Umbrella Facility for Gender Equality. Management also reported on its commitment to support gender through IDA, and defined specific goals and actions.

IEG rated the recommendations "substantial" for implementation in 2014, the last year of follow-up in the MAR, while noting areas that need more attention, such as further strengthening the results framework and not limiting outcome indicators to female beneficiaries.

Sources: IEG 2010; MAR of gender equality evaluation.

disproportionately provides financial services to women. In 2008 IFC included sex-disaggregated indicators in its Development Outcome Tracking System (DOTS) and, more recently, adopted a gender flag for Advisory and Investment Services.[3] In 2015 IFC proposed including a gender indicator in the IFC scorecard for FY16.

The analysis presented in this chapter shows that progress on gender integration at entry was not matched by similar attention to quality and depth, both in solidity of the approach and measurement of results. The emphasis on expanding gender integration at entry generated mixed results— attention to gender expanded, but the effort often became a mechanical approach (a box-ticking exercise) instead of meaningful and substantial integration. Current guidelines refer to integrating gender when relevant, but do not define "relevant," resulting in variable practice. Poor measurement persists because the gender flag guidelines are largely process-oriented and do not address more substantive issues, such as results measurement. Projects and country strategies do not sufficiently consider factors that are crucial for achieving impact, focusing attention mostly on elements considered important for integration at entry (which may not be as important for generating results).

Some of the same drawbacks identified above were noted by Bank Group staff interviewed for the analysis to prepare the MAR 2013 update on implementation of the recommendations of the 2010 gender evaluation. Among challenges interviewees cited were:[4] a perception that gender work is not very relevant and adds little value; data gaps and poor linkages between analytical and operational needs and data requirements; an excessively process-oriented approach that often translates into lip-service and bean-counting rather than substantial integration; lack of resources, including skills related to injecting gender knowledge into projects, programs, and strategies; low demand by client countries; and the risk that gender may be a "passing phase" in the institution.

The analysis in this RAP could not rely on a corporate definition of success beyond the quantitative indicators that are part of the Corporate Scorecards. Therefore, it focuses on dimensions of gender integration that can help define a qualitative benchmark:

- The definition of when (and why) addressing gender issues in projects and country strategies is relevant (with implications for coverage and targets for scaling up)

- Articulation of a results chain for gender, which demands achieving a coherent framework flowing from background analysis, to actions and components, to indicators and results (in country strategies this includes clarification of the value added of gender integration beyond purely mirroring gender integration in the country projects portfolio)

- Selection of appropriate indicators to measure results, and ensuring that results are accurately reported.

The analysis addresses two questions: What is the current approach adopted by the World Bank Group to integrate gender in operations and country strategies? To what extent do monitoring and evaluation (M&E) systems measure and report on gender results in operations and country strategies? The analysis is based on the following:

- A sample of 231 investment lending operations that closed in FY12 and FY14 (selected because they were previously screened by the IEG Gender Evaluation 2010)

- 190 IFC Advisory Services evaluated by IFC in FY12–14[5]

- 226 IFC investment operations self-evaluated by IFC and validated by IEG in FY12–14

- All 58 country strategies that closed in FY12–14

- Corporate documents

- Findings from recent IEG evaluations.

See appendix C for an explanation of the methodology used.[6]

The analysis does not focus on the actual results achieved or the effectiveness of World Bank Group support in achieving greater gender equality, and it is not an update of IEG's 2010 Gender Evaluation or a process evaluation. Its focus is on whether or not the system produces information that adequately reflects the quality and depth of gender integration, and whether current practice and the information it produces can effectively document results achieved in addressing gender issues in client countries.

A major goal of the first World Bank Group gender strategy is to focus more strongly on results at both the project and country strategy level.[7] The new strategy, *World Bank Group Gender Strategy (FY16–23): Gender Equality, Poverty Reduction, and Inclusive Growth* (World Bank 2015), emphasizes the importance of a country-based approach, and links the gender equality agenda to the World Bank Group's Twin Goals. This analysis aims to inform all stakeholders, and to assist the World Bank Group and particularly the Gender CCSA in strengthening the approach to documenting, assessing, and evaluating results during rollout of the new strategy.

Are projects and country strategies gender informed?

Integration of gender in projects (whether gender issues were considered and addressed) has been traditionally tracked along three dimensions: in the underlying analysis, in the actions proposed, or in M&E arrangements. A gender flag for systematically tracking integration at entry formalized this approach in FY13.[8] At the time, a project qualified as gender informed if just one dimension was present; since FY15, all three dimensions must be present to qualify. Gender integration in country strategies is not flagged, but is tracked using essentially the same approach. The flag is mandatory for IBRD and IDA projects, but only at entry (the appraisal stage); the task team leader (TTL) self-assigns the flag, and there is no requirement for the three dimensions to connect to one another or to the operation's development objectives.

The approach to defining and tracking gender-informed projects provides a relatively static and disconnected picture of gender integration that does not allow for thorough assessment of quality or intent, and does not reveal the expected or actual results (there are no inclusion criteria for the indicators selected). Table 1.1 shows the results of applying the gender-informed flag to the sample of IBRD and IDA projects used in this analysis. Half of the projects reviewed addressed gender in at least one of the three dimensions—the smallest set is projects integrating or explicitly planning to integrate gender indicators at the outcome or output level. One-fourth of all projects integrated gender in all three dimensions, though not necessarily linked in a common framework.

Fifty of the 58 country strategies analyzed for this report (all those that closed during FY12–14, 35 of which were joint World Bank–IFC strategies) touched on gender issues in diagnostics, actions, or pillars (Table 1.2).[9] Twenty-one percent of country strategies analyzed had gender present in all three dimensions as currently required (analysis, content, and results framework). This is lower than the rate reported in official documents. According to the Corporate Scorecard, in FY15 all country strategies integrated gender (meeting the target of 100 percent satisfactory attention to gender two years before the FY17 deadline).[10] The "Update on the Implementation of the Gender Equality Agenda at the World Bank Group" (World Bank 2012) reported that 57 percent of IDA country strategies integrated gender in three dimensions in FY11 and 86 percent did so in FY12 (p. 24, table 1). (Figures were not reported for non-IDA country strategies, which normally integrate gender at lower rates.)

Undoubtedly a strong effort was made between FY11 and FY13 to ensure that country strategies integrated gender (especially in IDA countries, due to IDA commitments). This is reflected in a dramatic increase in gender integration from the previous period (when the country strategies in the sample were approved, around FY08–09). At the same time, there have never been specific requirements regarding the quality of this integration, for example the dimensions of gender integration being coherently linked to one another and to the rest of the strategy. Of the 58 country strategies examined, 23 included gender in their objectives and pillars: five addressed gender in a pillar and 18 addressed it in a cross-cutting way.

IFC's approach, unlike the World Bank's, is highly selective and defined around specific gender private sector dimensions. IFC's priorities for gender integration center on fostering women's roles in five areas corresponding to a limited portion of the IFC portfolio: entrepreneurship, employment,

TABLE 1.1 | Integration of Gender in IBRD and IDA Projects, FY12–14

Projects (n=231)	Percent
Gender in background or analysis	47
Gender actions in actions or components	43
Gender in M&E	29
Gender in at least one dimension	56
Gender in three dimensions: analysis, actions, and M&E	24

Source: IEG calculation based on projects portfolio review.
Note: M&E = monitoring and evaluation.

TABLE 1.2 | Integration of Gender in Country Strategies, FY12–14

Country strategies (n=58)	Percent
Gender in background or analysis	48
Gender actions in objectives or pillars	40
Gender in M&E	50
Gender in at least one dimension	86
Gender in three dimensions: analysis, pillars, and M&E	21
Gender included in a cross-cutting way	31

Source: IEG calculation based on country strategy portfolio review.
Note: M&E = monitoring and evaluation.

corporate leadership, customers, and consumers. Gender is virtually absent from business lines or sectors that were not priorities for gender. In 2015 IFC selected agriculture, extractives, and finance as sectors of specific gender focus and set targets for gender results in these sectors in the IFC Scorecard. Table 1.3 shows that the share of Advisory Services projects with gender objectives is small and in some cases nonexistent. Investment Services does not have clear-cut objectives. Both Advisory and Investment Services, however, can address gender issues through project activities (the last section and Table 1.6 show Advisory Services activities). A few Access to Finance projects specifically target women borrowers and are required to collect sex-disaggregated indicators of outreach. Similarly to what happens for the Bank, though, gender is more frequently addressed through project activities than in project objectives.

Rationale and relevance for gender integration need to be more explicitly stated

Just because projects or country strategies integrate gender at entry, per World Bank Group policies, does not mean they clearly articulate a rationale for addressing gender issues. Commonly, projects and country strategies that discuss gender issues or even identify gender indicators do not clearly define the goal of gender integration. Although policy does not require defining the goal, the lack of an explicit rationale for gender integration often results in ambiguities in the proposed approach, and in a poorly developed or missing results chain that defines how gender results would be achieved. Should reducing specific gender inequalities be the rationale, or should gender issues be analyzed and addressed whenever they represent key constraints or bottlenecks in achieving project or country strategy goals? Should there be a distinct objective aiming to address specific gender issues or should gender be integrated across several objectives as a cross-cutting, contributory element—or both? Furthermore, should *all* projects and country strategies integrate gender?

TABLE 1.3 | Integration of Gender in IFC Projects, FY12–14

	Total projects		Projects with gender objectives	
	Number	Percent	Number	Percent
Investment Services	**226**	**100**	**n.a.**	**n.a.**
Manufacturing, agribusiness, and services	82	36	n.a.	n.a.
Infrastructure and natural resources	36	16	n.a.	n.a.
Financial institutions group	70	31	n.a.	n.a.
Telecommunications, media, technology, and venture capital	38	17	n.a.	n.a.
Advisory Services	**190**	**100**	**13**	**12**
Access to finance	63	33	5	8
Investment climate	41	22	2	5
Public-private partnership	24	13	0	0
Sustainable business advisory	62	33	6	10

Source: IEG calculation based on IFC portfolio review.
Note: n.a. = not applicable.

The expectation in the Corporate Scorecard's targets is that all country strategies should include gender. The country-driven approach to gender justifies this target; the approach requires that objectives be set at the country level and respond to the local context. According to World Bank operational policy, country strategies should draw on and discuss the findings of a gender diagnostic. Systematic Country Diagnostics are required to incorporate gender in their analytical frameworks starting in FY16. As for projects, the target set for FY17 is for 66 percent of projects to integrate gender in three dimensions—this target is based on a realistic assessment, given the current baseline, as opposed to expressing an ideal goal of what the profile of World Bank Group lending should generate.[11] Regardless of whether universal coverage should or should not be the aim, only an explicit discussion of why addressing gender issues is relevant in the context of that country strategy (or project) can allow robust articulation of a results chain, prioritization of actions, identification of expected results and corresponding indicators to measure them, and definition of the relevant portfolio (which may be less than 100 percent of the Bank's projects).

Although quantitative targets for country strategies and IBRD and IDA projects are highly ambitious, no specific standards are defined regarding quality aspects—the why (relevance) and the how (approach, design, result chain) of gender integration. Most country strategies and World Bank projects refer to or discuss gender-related issues, but most do not present a logical chain that links background analysis, actions, pillars or components, and indicators. Hence, complying with corporate requirements does not guarantee substantial integration. It is possible for a project document or country strategy to include all three dimensions required by the flag, but the dimensions may be unrelated to each other, to the main objectives of the project or strategy, or both. Coherence, or lack of it, is not captured by the gender flag.

IEG's analysis shows that the rationale for including at least some discussion of gender-related issues in project documents is usually unclear. Project documents often refer broadly to one or more priority gender issues at the country level, but tend not to provide detail on the implications of project activities for males and females. Because advancing gender equality is almost never the central goal of Bank projects, it is reasonable to expect some discussion in project documentation of how the project will integrate gender aspects—for example, a discussion of transmission channels, different behavioral responses expected, potential trade-offs and expected or unexpected impacts, or desired results. Such detail is rare. Instead of helping project teams develop a clear rationale for addressing gender issues in a project, the gender flag system fosters the urgency to comply by supporting the implicit notion that gender should be relevant by default.

Most operations may have a differential impact on men and women, and boys and girls, but some may not. Therefore, more guidance is needed on how to identify projects that should be considered relevant for, or more conducive to, gender integration. To help better understand and explain practice, IEG analyzed relevance by grouping Bank projects into five categories:[12]

1. Projects that actively **aim to address gender inequalities and biases** as their main goal (for example, supporting female entrepreneurship, expanding publicly funded care, interventions introducing protective legislation to address gender-based violence, and so on)

2. Projects that may have the **potential to positively impact gender inequalities and biases** and could introduce or modify activities to effect that change (for example, community-driven development projects promoting female participation and empowerment)

3. Projects that may have the **potential to damage gender relationships or worsen biases** and could introduce mitigation measures to avoid it (for example, projects identifying the risk of triggering domestic violence)

4. Projects that may take advantage of **behavioral differences** to amplify their impact (for example, conditional cash transfer (CCT) projects targeting women as recipients of the benefit), which may reduce or amplify gaps

5. Projects that do **not immediately and directly impact gender inequalities** (for example, introduction of computers in ministries, privatization of financial institutions, and so on).

Based on this classification,[13] 173 projects were relevant for gender inclusion (categories 1 to 4), or 75 percent of the total sample of 231 investment lending projects reviewed. Two percent of projects—mostly health projects with the goal of reducing maternal mortality—directly aimed to address gender inequalities (category 1). Category 2 accounted for the largest proportion of projects overall (66 percent). Category 3 accounted for 6 percent of projects—mostly infrastructure projects involving resettlements.

Only one project was in category 4, which may be partly explained by the low number of social protection projects in the sample (including conditional cash transfer). Projects not relevant for gender (category 5) were 25 percent of the sample. Even though gender was remotely relevant in this last group, project documentation commonly includes some discussion on gender, especially at closing.

When reexamining gender integration using the five proposed categories, not all projects that could include a gender dimension actually did (Table 1.4). Of the 173 projects relevant from a gender integration perspective, 100 integrated gender in actions or components.[14] Thirty-two percent included gender in all three dimensions, and 74 percent addressed it in at least one dimension. Only 10 projects (6 percent of all gender-relevant ones) explicitly included gender in the project development objective (PDO).

A modest 62 percent of gender-relevant projects included some discussion of gender issues in the Project Appraisal Document or referred to relevant analytical work on gender. Projects do not take the best advantage of consultations during project preparation, and consultations seldom contribute to defining the gender relevance of interventions. About 50 percent of the Project Appraisal Documents reviewed indicated that gender consultations occurred, but only half of those discussed the implications of the consultations for project design. Without an explicit discussion of the relevance of gender to the project's main objectives, important dimensions may be overlooked, as is clearly illustrated by the findings of recent IEG thematic evaluations (Box 1.2).[15]

Projects rarely defined the relevance of gender integration (the why), and even more rarely discussed the gender results chain (the how) to develop and motivate their gender-specific design features. To be internally coherent, the gender results chain must be grounded in the core results chain of the project and establish the relationship between gender aspects and project activities. That is why defining relevance is an important prelude to defining the results chain.[16] However, project documentation rarely discussed gender relevance. Only 11 projects clearly defined and explained why addressing gender issues was important for achieving project objectives. There were no discussions of why gender was not relevant, or

TABLE 1.4 | **Integration of Gender in IBRD and IDA Gender-Relevant Projects, FY12–14**

Projects (n=231)	Percent
Gender in background or analysis	62
Gender actions in actions or components	58
Gender in M&E	39
Gender in at least one dimension	74
Gender in three dimensions: analysis, actions, and M&E	32

Source: IEG calculation based on projects portfolio review.
Note: M&E = monitoring and evaluation.

Box 1.2 | Findings from Recently Completed IEG Thematic Evaluations

The lack of an explicit discussion of gender relevance often results in poor integration of gender in areas where integration is expected, as illustrated in recent IEG thematic evaluations.

The early childhood development evaluation (IEG 2015e) found that the World Bank's work on gender and early childhood development did not establish synergies between them. Bank-supported early childhood development interventions do not seem to recognize the crucial role these interventions have in relieving constraints to the labor market participation of parents and especially women. Furthermore, Bank-supported early childhood development interventions do not address parents' vital role in stimulating children's development, and the importance of providing parent support programs.

The investment climate evaluation (IEG 2015b) found that explicitly targeting women entrepreneurs as a category deserving specific attention is uncommon, even in projects that more directly impact small entrepreneurs and the constraints more likely to affect women (for example, reforms dealing with registering property, land administration, permits, tax regulations, agriculture, licensing, access to land, and property rights). A close analysis of projects that target women entrepreneurs revealed that many projects are small and focused mostly on capacity-building activities, or on filling an information gap related to gender-based barriers in the business-enabling environment. Most of those projects target women as participants in training or consultative working groups instead of entrepreneurs (or potential entrepreneurs) who are supposed to benefit directly from investment climate reforms.

The evaluation of World Bank Group support to low-income fragile and conflict-affected situations (FCSs; IEG 2013g) found that the Bank paid insufficient attention to conflict-related violence against women and economic empowerment of women in low-income FCSs. Measures to address the effects of conflict-related violence against women or to promote women's economic empowerment during reconstruction were almost absent in World Bank Group projects and country strategies in these states. The evaluation pointed to the lack of gender-sensitive actions in state building and in most of the demobilization, disarmament, and reintegration programs in fragile and conflict-affected situations.

why the team decided not to integrate gender in the project design. The IEG social safety nets and gender report (IEG 2014) found that programs are sometimes ambiguous in the type of gender elements they include and the reasons for including them—they rarely analyze the motivations, underlying results chain, and crucial contextual elements. Specifically, it is rare to find an explicit discussion of the assumptions about gender roles and responsibilities in the household and the community.

The three dimensions defined by the flag (diagnostic, actions, and indicators) are not always aligned in projects that include all three of them. The reason is that many projects at the Project Appraisal Document stage generically define activities, or include specific activities but no corresponding indicators. IEG's analysis found that only half of the projects that had diagnostic, actions, and indicators achieved substantive coherence—actions and activities clearly motivated by pertinent diagnostic work and measured using appropriate indicators.

Findings of the recent IEG financial inclusion evaluation (IEG 2015a) illustrate the importance of broadly articulating a results chain for gender. The evaluation found that gender was included when relevant—that is, gender was generally an important dimension in financial inclusion projects in countries with low inclusion rates for women (the focus on gender aligned with the needs). However, less than 3 percent of projects provided detailed information about targeted women, despite explicit reference to women as beneficiaries in about one-third of Bank Group–supported financial inclusion projects. Furthermore, the evaluation found that financial inclusion projects frequently fail to address constraints specific to women beneficiaries.

IFC's approach to gender integration is more focused, but has lower coverage

For three of the five private sector dimensions it identified as priorities—entrepreneurship, employment, and corporate leadership—IFC outlined the rationale for focusing on women and gender issues and articulated a gender results chain (a business case for investing in women) through developing specific initiatives. For example, since 2007 IFC has supported the Global Banking Alliance for Women, a program launched in 2000 that aims to promote women's entrepreneurship through building the capacity of financial institutions to serve women customers. IFC launched SheWorks in 2014, a private sector partnership to improve employment opportunities for women. In the same year, the Goldman Sachs Foundation's 10,000 Women initiative and IFC launched the **Women Entrepreneurs Opportunity Facility that is dedicated exclusively to financing women-owned small and medium enterprises (SMEs) in developing countries.** Each initiative focused on a concrete approach to address specific barriers for women, such as legal and financial barriers impeding women-owned enterprises from developing into larger-scale, job-generating firms, or barriers in the labor market that tend to keep women in the informal economy instead of salaried work. IFC strategy involved clients in the piloting phase or partnerships (such as 10,000 Women)[17] to ensure buy-in and the adoption of best practices.

The IFC approach to integrating gender involves defining relevance and a results chain at the level of the program rather than the level of the operation. Therefore, it is a more standardized approach relying on implementation teams to tailor it to local needs and individual project contexts.

The approach to gender integration differs between Advisory Services and Investment Services. Among Investment Services, Banking on Women projects (providing women-owned businesses with access to finance) are virtually the only ones with a gender objective (Table 1.3), although other projects may include gender activities. The percentage of Advisory Services projects that gave high attention to gender, based on the IFC gender flag, did not change much between FY08 and FY14 (about 5 percent of the portfolio). However, the percentage of projects reporting some attention to gender (including through project activities), even if small (less than 25 percent of total expenses) has more than doubled between FY12 and FY14, reaching 25 percent of the Advisory Services portfolio. The IFC Road Maps FY14–16 (IFC 2013) and FY15–17 (IFC 2014) state that Advisory Services will contribute to all IFC priorities with emphasis on gender, among others.

Since gender-focused banking initiatives were introduced in the financial sector in 2007, IFC has deployed packages of Investment and Advisory Services to financial institutions aiming to develop and grow banking products for women entrepreneurs.[18] IEG validated several such projects as part of the Global Entrepreneurship Markets initiative and found that these early pilots, implemented in Africa, introduced new products and resulted in sustained lending to women entrepreneurs by client financial institutions even after the IFC project closed. They also had demonstration effects on financial institutions launching new lending products to women in local markets. Attempting to build on this success, efforts to mainstream gender into African programs for micro, small, and medium-sized enterprise programs struggled to adapt to local client needs and market realities. Of seven Advisory Services projects closed in FY14, six dropped gender components and one project failed. A major lesson of the approach is that programs need to be tailored to the needs and capacity of local subsidiaries and to local market conditions.[19]

Evaluated advisory projects with gender-relevant information are mostly concentrated in IFC's Access to Finance and Sustainable Business Advisory business lines (Table 1.3). A small number of these projects are exclusively gender-focused, but more often gender is one objective of many. The most common gender references found in Advisory Services projects related to supporting women entrepreneurs and female-owned SMEs, creating jobs for women, expanding access to finance, and opening more opportunities for women to serve on company boards—all of which are in line with IFC's women-focused programs. Of 190 Advisory Services projects analyzed, 13 (7 percent) had gender objectives, and 33 (17 percent) had gender-relevant activities. Training was the activity most frequently delivered by projects.

Most microfinance initiatives were joint efforts between Investment Services and Advisory Services. Some had gender objectives, but most aimed to provide incentives to microfinance institution clients to meet gender targets in their lending instead of implementing concrete gender-relevant activities (such as developing new products for women entrepreneurs or capacity-building activities). Two of 41 Investment Climate projects had gender objectives; one was a Special Economic Zone initiative aimed to promote policies benefitting women zone workers, the other was an Alternative Dispute Mechanism project supporting the inclusion of women in mediation, with targets for training delivery to women and cases solved through mediation. Finally, six of 62 former Sustainable Business Advisory projects had gender objectives; of these projects three were SME-farmer linkage projects with IFC investment clients (focused on including women in training only), and one was a corporate governance project targeting women-owned firms and increasing the number of women on corporate boards. No public-private partnership projects had gender objectives, even though one project flagged women as major beneficiaries; that project did not try to track women beneficiaries in its indicators.

Unlike the World Bank, which has no gender safeguard or performance standard related to gender, IFC has gender-related requirements in its Sustainability Framework[20] and Performance Standards (IFC 2012b). IFC's clients are required to comply with applicable requirements of the Performance Standards, while in advisory activities IFC provides advice consistent with the Performance Standards. The update to the IFC Sustainability Framework, effective January 1, 2012 (IFC 2012a), strengthened IFC's commitment to gender and stated, "IFC believes that women have a crucial role to play in achieving sound economic growth and poverty reduction. They are essential part of private sector development. IFC expects its clients to minimize gender-related risks from business activities and unintended gender differentiated impacts. Recognizing that women are often prevented from realizing their economic potential because of gender inequity, IFC is committed to creating opportunities for women through its investment and advisory activities." (IFC 2012a, p. 3.)

IFC addresses gender in multiple Performance Standards. Performance Standard 1, Assessment and Management of Environmental and Social Risks and Impacts, requires the client to identify individuals and groups that may be affected by the project because of their vulnerable status and, if so, adopt differentiated measures to mitigate those adverse impacts.[21] Performance Standard 2, Labor and Working Conditions, requires the client to promote fair treatment of workers and non-discrimination and equal opportunity in the workplace. In particular, the client needs to prevent and address harassment, intimidation, and exploitation especially of women. Performance Standard 5, Land Acquisition and Involuntary Resettlement, requires the client to ensure that women's circumstances are not worsened by the project in relation to the pre-project situation and to raise the profile of gender-related matters in discussions with government agencies and other relevant groups during resettlement planning, in order to encourage more equitable treatment of affected women. Performance Standard 7, Indigenous People, requires that the client assess and document potential impacts on indigenous people. Specifically, the assessment of land and natural resource use should be gender-inclusive and consider women's roles in the management and use of these resources.

At present, IFC does not systematically collect data on gender; nor does it monitor IFC commitments or the client's commitments on gender aspects of projects or programs.

Selecting gender as a cross-cutting theme dilutes the focus in country strategies

Gender is integrated in country strategies more frequently as a cross-cutting theme than as a stand-alone pillar or component. This occurs for a number of reasons. Country strategies are required to be selective, realistic, and strategic in their definition of objectives and have to balance the country's development challenges and goals with the Bank Group's goals and comparative advantage. The number of pillars is limited to three or four per strategy, and the pillars tend to be broadly defined (for example, social inclusion, growth). Hence, it would be unrealistic to expect a pillar solely devoted to gender. Furthermore, gender is inherently cross-cutting and relevant for many sectors and themes.

Fifty of the 58 country strategies that closed between FY12 and FY14 (86 percent) incorporated gender in at least some dimension. However, the percentage drops substantially when applying the stricter requirement of providing a logical chain, or alignment, among diagnostics, actions, and M&E. Only 55 percent of country strategy documents that identified or diagnosed gender issues addressed gender in objectives, pillars, or actions.

The integration of gender as a cross-cutting issue or as part of a pillar does not necessarily result in gender issues being addressed through present or planned operations, and it does not result in the inclusion of appropriate indicators to monitor results. Six country strategies (10 percent) clearly identified or programmed a gender-relevant lending operation (one country strategy also referred to accompanying analytical work) and set up corresponding indicators—that is, they were internally consistent (Figure 1.1). Twelve other country strategies referred to planned or in-progress analytical work on gender. Only one country strategy (Pakistan) referred to technical assistance work on gender.[22]

None of the 18 country strategies that defined gender as a cross-cutting issue explained what that designation meant operationally. Country strategies that opted for gender as a cross-cutting issue effectively avoided any discussion of the rationale for gender integration in specific pillars or strategic objectives. Instead, the discussion of rationale was handed over to the current and future portfolios, without elaborating on how the strategy itself added value in moving the gender agenda forward. As reported by poverty assessment leads and country economists interviewed for the evaluation of poverty

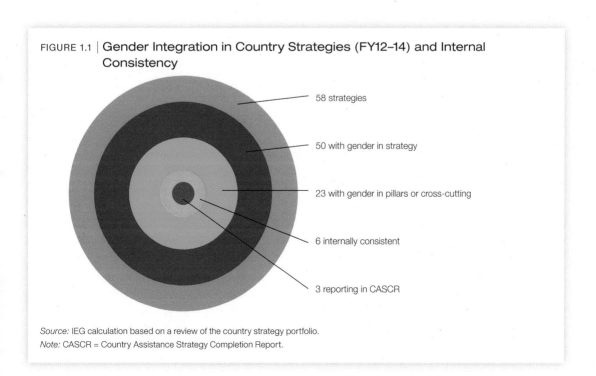

FIGURE 1.1 | Gender Integration in Country Strategies (FY12–14) and Internal Consistency

- 58 strategies
- 50 with gender in strategy
- 23 with gender in pillars or cross-cutting
- 6 internally consistent
- 3 reporting in CASCR

Source: IEG calculation based on a review of the country strategy portfolio.
Note: CASCR = Country Assistance Strategy Completion Report.

in country programs (IEG 2015c), issues such as gender and shared prosperity are included in country strategies because they may be current trends in the World Bank and are merely used to tick a box.

In three of the five strategies that identified gender as an objective within a specific pillar, the objective was to improve access to health and education services for women or girls (Nicaragua, Niger, and Senegal). In Timor-Leste, the objective was to improve the capacity to monitor results in the field, with particular attention to women and youth under a governance pillar (but no specific corresponding action). The Ethiopia country strategy contained a cross-cutting objective, though it was embedded in an individual pillar (mainstreaming gender considerations in all lending PDOs).

Even when country strategies had a gender-specific objective, they did not necessarily discuss how achieving that particular objective would contribute to achieving the overall goals of the country strategy. Twenty-three of the country strategies reviewed (40 percent) specified at least one gender issue among the country development priorities; however, none of the 159 pillars in the country strategies reviewed addressed gender issues. Only five of the 559 associated strategic objectives reviewed focused on gender. None of these cases discussed how the gender objectives were selected based on the diagnostic work or consultations, how they related to the other objectives of the country strategy, and how achievement was going to be assessed beyond the actual delivery of the referenced economic and sector work or operation.

IDA country strategies had a higher level of gender integration than those of non-IDA countries. All five of the country strategy documents that included an explicit gender pillar were IDA countries, as were 90 percent of the country strategies where gender was explicitly integrated in a cross-cutting manner (IDA countries represented 65 percent of the country strategies reviewed). Joint World Bank–IFC strategies did not show a higher level of gender integration.

The overall majority of gender-related actions outlined in country strategies were women-specific. Jamaica is the only exception among 58 country strategies reviewed. That strategy had a special focus on boys in education, school-to-work transition, and skills development projects or technical assistance.

Details of consultations that can help identify where gender is a priority were scarce or absent in country strategy documents. In the few cases where there was information (38 percent of the country strategies reviewed provided some information on gender consultations), consultations tended to be with civil society organizations (including women's groups), but rarely involved the private sector or government. Gender consultations were more often reported in IDA countries, but interestingly, country strategies with gender in pillars were not more likely to include details on gender consultations than those integrating gender as a cross-cutting theme.

Consultations did not necessarily influence the country strategy. Women's empowerment issues (political participation, participation in labor markets, and access to finance) were recurring topics during consultations conducted in preparation for country strategies, yet these topics were rarely selected as gender priorities in country strategies. Only four country strategies (Ethiopia, Jordan, Nicaragua, and Tunisia) outlined a plan to respond to the issues raised during the consultations.

Indicators used to track gender results are generally inadequate

Indicators used in country strategies and projects were generally inadequate to capture gender results. When present, indicators were narrow in scope and tended to measure outputs instead of outcomes. Often they were not well defined and were insufficient to establish attribution.[23] IEG's analysis shows that few of the PDO indicators captured gender gaps and their evolution, gender inequality measures, or gender biases. Most indicators used were core sector indicators. Projects increasingly report on female beneficiaries, but this indicator is not always helpful, especially when it refers to project recipients or residents of the project area. Even when technically feasible, strategies and projects often did not sex-disaggregate person-level project indicators. Box 1.3 reports several examples of output indicators used in place of outcome indicators, as well as of poorly defined, unmeasurable indicators. Reporting on the indicators was typically sound when indicators were integrated at an early stage and were grounded in concrete actions and components. Selecting indicators when designing the project (which requires the early definition of a results chain for gender) may be crucial to ensuring that results are better captured.

Reporting of gender results was generally poor, especially in country strategies. This is partially explained by unclear requirements regarding reporting of gender results when gender is integrated in country strategies as a cross-cutting theme. IEG's analysis also found that when specific gender objectives were not part of a pillar, reporting (when it happened) tended to focus on the activities that occurred during the strategy period, using output indicators.

Gender indicators in country strategies focus on outputs

Gender indicators used in country strategies are typically intermediate in nature and output level, and based on project-level indicators. Some country strategies even include input indicators in their results framework (such as the number of condoms distributed, or the outreach of the program). Output indicators—and input indicators even less so—are not sufficient to document gender results, particularly because the objectives outlined in country strategies are typically expressed as development outcomes.

This finding is consistent with the more general finding highlighted in IEG evaluations: that results frameworks in country strategies mostly focus on outputs instead of outcomes; weak links exist between designed interventions and outcomes; and monitoring indicators to track outcomes are often missing.[24] A problem that is not unique to gender but affects gender in particular is that pillars and objectives outlined in country strategies tend to be broad, while indicators are much more specific because they are often selected from the project results framework. Because gender is never a pillar of the strategy, it is represented, at most, by one or two indicators that are insufficient to capture the more general objectives mentioned in the strategy.

Regarding the selection of gender indicators, there is also a clear preference for human development indicators in projects and country strategies. Almost half of the gender indicators in the 58 country strategies reviewed were either education or reproductive and maternal health indicators. Similarly, most projects with

Box 1.3 | Indicators in Projects and Country Strategies

Indicators used in country strategies and projects were generally inadequate to capture gender results for two main reasons. First, output indicators were often used to measure development outcomes in projects and country strategies. Some examples:

- Percentage of pregnant women receiving a prophylactic treatment during the pregnancy

- Percentage of pregnant women receiving (or reporting consumption of) iron and folate

- Number of women applicants using land deeds to obtain access to credit

- Increase in female farmers registered in farmer-based organizations

- Number of female beneficiaries of public works programs supported under the project

- Share of rural producers who are women receiving technical assistance to increase land productivity

- Increase in the share of schools equipped with sanitation facilities

- HIV testing and access to mother-to-child-transmission prevention programs

- Number of proposals submitted by women and number funded

- Percentage of women participating in the program

- Share of trained teachers

- Number of pregnant women living with HIV who received anti-retroviral therapy to reduce the risk of mother-to-child transmission

- Number of sub-projects of which women are the main beneficiaries

- Presence of women in village committees

- Number of girls and other disadvantaged children covered by incentives schemes

- Number of male and female condoms distributed

- Number of beneficiary households, disaggregated by gender, income level, and ethnic minority

- Number of pregnant/lactating women, adolescent girls and/or children under age five reached by basic nutrition services.

Box 1.3 | Indicators in Projects and Country Strategies *(continued)*

The second reason why indicators were inadequate was that they were poorly defined, that is, they were not expressed as measurable indicators. Some examples:

- Increased voice of the poor and women within communities resulting in better targeting of local investments

- Education and skills development aligned with knowledge economy and employment needs; Improving the quality of education and training for both women and men

- Options for safety nets are examined and acted on to support disabled and elderly people, pregnant women and new mothers, street and working children, and others who are vulnerable

- Increased rights awareness among women and disseminated knowledge on social protection

- Increased awareness of girls' education through training provided to school management committees

- Increased number of entrepreneurial jobs, especially for women and youth

- Enhanced cognitive, emotional, language, social, and physical development of boys and girls completing kindergarten

- Improved learning outcomes in rural and ethnic minority areas.

Source: IEG analysis of project documents and country strategies.

gender indicators were in education and health; the indicators often measured access or coverage, and quality more rarely. Few indicators measured gender dimensions of employment and entrepreneurship, or of agricultural and rural development. Essentially absent were indicators of voice and agency.[25]

Reporting on the indicators was typically sound in the few cases in which gender actions were identified and were supported by a relevant background diagnostic, and indicators were integrated into Country Assistance Strategy (CAS) programs. This is the case in four of five country strategies that included gender at the pillar level, and in 13 out of 18 where gender was integrated in a cross-cutting way (for at least one indicator reported). Similarly, projects generally reported on PDO-level gender indicators when they were included in projects. The Implementation Completion and Results (ICR) generally tracked and reported on the majority of PDO-level gender indicators included in relevant Project Appraisal Documents (69 percent). Interestingly, some projects not considered to be gender-relevant (at least at entry) reported some results on gender.

Unlike projects, completion reports for country strategies do not have a section dedicated to gender results to facilitate more systematic reporting. Reporting tends to focus on the activities that occurred during the strategy period without linking the activities with the overall Country Assistance Strategy outcomes (including the gender aspects of those outcomes) to which they are supposedly contributing. Country strategies tend to list individual interventions or pieces of analytical work that have some gender element (typically related to women's issues), but there is no effort to connect the individual pieces to the strategic objectives. The focus tends to be on the project instead of the strategic-level impact. Indonesia is a good example. Despite reporting on a number of women-focused activities as part of the financing and analytic and policy advice work in labor markets, the strategy failed to articulate a common goal encompassing the collective learning and to provide evidence of the strategy's value added. This is a common deficit in the analytical work. Several strategies discussed gender in planned analytical work, but the reporting is limited to the accountability part (whether a study was or was not conducted), with no discussion of the application or impacts of that work.

Even when gender is an objective of a pillar, reporting of gender results may not occur. The Timor-Leste country strategy included gender in its governance pillar and as a cross-cutting theme. However, reporting on the results achieved was so scattered that IEG noted in its Country Assostance Strategy Completion Report Review: "Mainstreaming an issue (for example, youth, gender, and governance) is increasingly used in CAS design to highlight its importance. In reality, however, this often results in diluted attention, weak support, and no accountability for achieving results. It is thus critically important to devote at least as much attention to building a strong results chain for the cross-cutting themes as to any other pillars, and include them in the results framework for proper tracking of progress."

Lessons learned from country strategies rarely capture gender results. Only five country strategy documents (9 percent) explicitly refer to gender in the lessons derived from previous Country Assistance Strategy Completion Reports.

IDA and IBRD projects do not identify gender relevance or articulate a results chain

Project results frameworks seldom include gender indicators to measure gender results. Twenty-nine percent of projects for which gender was a relevant dimension had PDO-level gender indicators;[26] one-third were added during implementation. Outcome indicators were scarce, but the two most common were maternal mortality ratio and HIV/AIDS prevalence (disaggregated by sex). Sixteen gender-relevant projects with no gender indicators stated the intention to track some gender dimension in their M&E (only two effectively did based on information reported when the project was completed). Another 50 projects refer to expected gender impacts in the Project Appraisal Document (mainly women's participation or access to services), but fail to include an indicator to track progress. Indicators may be added during implementation, though, because restructuring is an opportunity to strengthen attention to gender in a given project. A rural transport project in Vietnam is a good example. Through a dedicated gender fund the project added actions to the design to facilitate women's involvement and measure the impact on social and economic empowerment.[27] Twenty-eight percent of restructured projects in IEG's analysis added gender actions, indicators, or both.

Few PDO indicators captured gender inequality measures (except for gender parity in education, a core sector indicator), gender biases, or gender gaps and their evolution. Projects more often tracked sex-disaggregated outputs or outcomes (education enrollment or completion, learning outcomes, immunization rates, training received, and so on) or female-specific indicators, such as access to prenatal care or maternal mortality.

The female beneficiaries indicator was common, especially in recent projects reviewed for this report—21 projects either reported absolute levels or discussed the number of female beneficiaries reached by projects. Project documents are required to report the number or percentage of female beneficiaries since June 2009, and since FY14, the Corporate Scorecards track this indicator disaggregated by sex. Consequently, there was an increase in reporting this indicator for new projects, and a number of projects added the indicator at restructuring (as highlighted by IEG 2015d).[28] Number or percentage of female beneficiaries was the only gender indicator in 15 projects. Reporting for this indicator was sometimes not meaningful, for example, when female beneficiaries were 50 percent of all beneficiaries based on the composition of the total population in the project area. These findings resonate with those presented in IEG 2014e, which highlighted the challenges of measuring gender impacts in a meaningful way. Defining and counting female beneficiaries requires going beyond the mere concepts of recipients or project area residents and measuring both the direct and broader distributional impacts. The requirement of reporting on sex-disaggregated beneficiaries, however, may increase teams and country clients of the importance of tracking project results in a sex-disaggregated way. An agriculture project in Mauritania did not originally include any gender indicators, despite having specific actions aimed at supporting women's cooperatives. When collecting information on female beneficiaries became mandatory, at restructuring the project team collected and reported some sex-disaggregated results despite severe limitations on data availability. The ICR notes: "the gender reporting required by the Bank forced executing agencies to start distinguishing in their reporting between female and male farmers. This is a distinction which is uncommon in Mauritania and without prodding by the project would not have happened. Over time, insistence on gender reporting by the Bank and other donors can be expected to lead to a better understanding of this issue and of more targeted interventions in favor of women farmers in the future."

Several IEG evaluations and learning products highlighted the drawbacks in projects' M&E frameworks, especially regarding gender indicators. The evaluation of electricity access (IEG 2015d), for instance, stressed the need for improvement in key performance indicators for gender, calling for a clear definition of beneficiaries versus users (they may be different groups), tracking outputs and outcomes (not just headcount figures), and identifying measures of outcomes beyond access. Most projects limited themselves to tracking the number of female beneficiaries.

Most gender indicators were core sector indicators, such as primary school completion rate, gender parity index, and number of pregnant women receiving antenatal care.[29] Although core sector indicators allow for tracking results in a more homogeneous way across the institution, they do not, by definition, capture the more nuanced and granular results of an intervention. In that regard, relying only on core sector indicators may have the effect of limiting the ability to document impacts.

Even when it is technically feasible, projects infrequently sex-disaggregate person-level indicators, sometimes even when disaggregation is the more obvious and easy way to track results for males and females and document the impact of the project on gender equality.[30] Forty percent of the 173 projects relevant for gender integration would have benefitted from additional PDO gender indicators (that is, meaningful disaggregation of person-level indicators was possible, but not done). Sectors with the largest percentage of projects presenting sex-disaggregated indicators (human development, mainly education and health, as shown in Figure 1.2) also had the largest percentage of missed opportunities—person-level indicators that could have been disaggregated by sex, but were not. The youth employment evaluation (IEG 2013b) noted that the World Bank's lending and nonlending portfolios targeted young women and men equally, but little is known about how young women or men benefitted from this support. Furthermore, the evaluation stressed that the monitoring framework in the 90 projects it reviewed was weak in identifying benefits by gender and other distributional impacts. Only three projects had a gender emphasis in the objective, and of those, only one had followed through by targeting interventions to young women and collecting relevant indicators.

The ICR section titled *Poverty Impacts, Gender Aspects, and Social Development* is not systematically used (as required) to report results on gender, unless the project includes a gender indicator. Only half of the 50 projects with an expected gender result identified at entry (but no corresponding gender indicator) discussed achievements in this section. A rural community

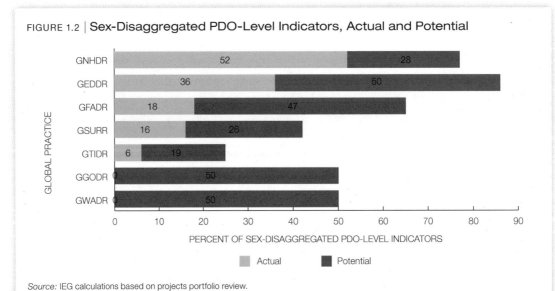

FIGURE 1.2 | **Sex-Disaggregated PDO-Level Indicators, Actual and Potential**

Source: IEG calculations based on projects portfolio review.
Note: "Actual" are PDO-level indicators that are currently sex-disaggregated. "Potential" are PDO-level indicators that could have been sex-disaggregated but were not (missed opportunity). GFADR= World Bank Agriculture Global Practice; GGODR = World Bank Governance Global Practice; GHNDR = World Bank Health, Nutrition, and Population Global Practice; GEDDR = World Bank Education Global Practice; GSURR= World Bank Social, Urban, Rural, and Resilience Global Practice; GTIDR = World Bank Transport and Information and Communication Technologies Global Practice; GWADR = World Bank Water Global Practice; PDO = project development objective.

development project in Mali is a good example of a project that, despite its lack of attention to gender at entry, provided good reporting on sex-disaggregated impacts at completion.[31] IEG also found reporting for 34 projects with no explicit gender results expected at entry. In most cases, results discussed in this section referred to the project's success in reaching women or girls. Generic statements were often included with regard to women's empowerment. The quality of the evidence reported is difficult to judge because the majority of project documents do not report sources to back up their statements. Some projects that did not refer to expected gender impacts at entry discuss positive impacts in this section that are plausible even if not supported by specific indicators (such as water projects that assumed women benefitted because of water connection).

Overall, qualitative reporting (for example, reporting of patterns observed or anecdotal evidence) is much more frequent than quantitative reporting (through quantitative indicators). This is consistent with the poor integration of gender indicators in M&E frameworks. Both qualitative and quantitative reporting have serious limitations, such as poorly reported indicators, vague qualitative statements, incoherent reporting, and not reporting indicators at all. The lessons learned rarely discuss results or lack of results regarding gender. This finding echoes one of the main messages highlighted by a recent report produced by the Agriculture Global Practice (Mollard and others 2015) as reported in Box 1.4.

Box 1.4 | Lessons from Tracking Results during Implementation in Agriculture

A recent report conducted by the World Bank Agriculture Global Practice is consistent with the findings presented in this chapter on the need to shift attention from gender integration at entry to how to track gender results during implementation and completion. The report reviewed 55 selected agriculture projects approved during FY08–13, and assessed whether they included concrete gender actions during project implementation and documented the impacts of those actions at closing. Key findings of the report are:

- Quality and extent of reporting on gender results varies considerably across projects

- Inconsistencies and weaknesses exist in the quality and quantity of indicators to track gender results

- Projects do not effectively use the dedicated section of the Implementation Completion and Results for reporting on gender results

- Agriculture operations underreport gender results, with subsequent loss of relevant lessons.

Source: Mollard and others 2015.

IFC projects have standard gender indicators, though the expected impact is unclear

IFC gender indicators are highly standardized and have been in the DOTS monitoring system since 2008. For Investment Services projects, four indicators are collected in a sex-disaggregated way: client's employment, students reached, women in corporate boards, and women in senior management positions.[32] The employment indicator is collected for most clients except financial institutions—Table 1.5 shows that 145 firms report direct sex-disaggregated employment data out of 156 that are required to report it). Even when these indicators are regularly collected (as is the case for the female employment indicator),[33] they do not capture the projects' expected development impacts. These DOTS indicators provide a profile of IFC clients but do not track results for end beneficiaries of IFC's projects, a general limitation and not related only to gender. Forty-two percent of staff surveyed for IEG's Biennial Report on Operations Evaluation (IEG 2013a) reported that there were many instances where the DOTS mandatory indicators were not sufficient to adequately reflect PDOs, which was also a challenge for assessing attributable results achievement.

By contrast, financial institutions are required to provide the number of customers (entrepreneurs) that held outstanding loans, and this indicator needs to be disaggregated by sex of the owner for Banking on Women and Blended Finance Program Clients (IFC established a methodology to define the sex of the owner or manager in SMEs). Although attribution is still difficult, the indicator "share of female entrepreneurs receiving loans from financial institutions" relates directly to the activities funded by the project. This indicator was collected by a few financial institutions as part of the expected results related to IFC's Development Goals (for both Investment Services and Advisory Services)—for example, Table 1.5 shows that five firms sex-disaggregated their portfolio of SMEs reached, and eight firms sex-disaggregated their microfinance portfolio. In some cases, the team did not originally plan to collect the access to finance indicator in a sex-disaggregated way, but did it at project completion.

For Advisory Services, each business line develops a logical results chain, including output, outcome, and impact indicators. Gender indicators are most often found in Financial Institutions Group and former Sustainable Business Advisory business lines (Table 1.6). Gender indicators mostly measure outputs instead of outcomes, and frequently track the number of women trained, or those participating in seminars, conferences, and specific initiatives. The relatively high number of projects with gender indicators partly reflects a percentage of projects with gender activities larger than those with gender objectives, as shown in Table 1.6.

Conclusion

The introduction of the gender strategy in 2001 signaled policy intent that has since resulted in wide-ranging efforts to integrate gender into World Bank Group practice, including, for example: requirements to integrate gender in country and project-level documentation, World Bank staff and team leader training, gender flags for the World Bank and IFC, and inclusion of gender indicators in IFC's DOTS. All of this effort and intent was to ensure meaningful engagement with gender issues and meaningful reporting on gender

TABLE 1.5 | Gender Indicators in DOTS for Investment Services, Frequency of Reporting by Business Line (Number of Projects and Firms Reporting)

	Access to finance for women					Women on boards	Women in top mgmt	Female employment			No gender indicators	Number of firms and projects
	Microf. loans	Microf. portfolio	SME portfolio	SME loans	Women reached			Total, direct	Direct contractors	Total, indirect		
Manufacturing, Agribusiness, and Services	–	–	–	–	–	2	–	78	3	6	4	82
Actual	–	–	–	–	–	2	–	68	3	6	4	–
Baseline only	–	–	–	–	–	–	–	10	–	–	–	–
Infrastructure and Natural Resources	–	–	–	–	–	6	7	31	–	1	5	36
Actual	–	–	–	–	–	4	5	27	–	1	5	–
Baseline only	–	–	–	–	–	2	2	4	–	–	–	–
Financial Institutions Group	6	8	5	2	1	11	–	1	–	–	48	70
Actual	6	8	4	1	1	9	–	1	–	–	48	–
Baseline only	–	–	1	1	–	2	–	–	–	–	–	–
Telecommunications, Media, Technology, and Venture Capital	–	–	–	–	–	–	3	35	–	–	2	38
Actual	–	–	–	–	–	–	2	30	–	–	2	–
Baseline only	–	–	–	–	–	–	1	5	–	–	–	–
Total	6	8	5	2	1	19	10	145	3	7	59	226

Source: IEG calculations based on DOTS data.

Note: DOTS = Development Outcome Tracking System; mgmt. = management; microf = microfinance; SME = small and medium enterprise.

TABLE 1.6 | Gender Objectives and Activities in Project Completion Reports, FY12–14

	PCRs		PCRs with gender objectives		PCRs with gender activities		PCRs with M&E indicators (outcome or output level)	
	Number	Percent	Number	Percent	Number	Percent	Number	Percent
Access to finance	63	33	5	8	12	19	32	51
Investment climate	41	22	2	5	7	17	20	49
Public-private partnership	24	13	0	0	0	0	0	0
Sustainable business advisory	62	33	6	10	14	23	39	63
Total	190	100	13	12	33	17	91	48

Source: IEG calculation based on Advisory Services portfolio review.
Note: M&E = monitoring and evaluation; PCR = project completion report.

integration; however, based on an analysis of projects and country strategies that recently closed, the findings documented in this chapter show that the result achieved so far is not convincing.

The analysis undertaken identifies three key areas that have not yet been recognized and addressed. First, there is currently no guidance to define when gender issues are relevant for projects to address and how to establish a categorization of projects based on relevance for gender integration. Prioritization may be required to achieve more meaningful gender integration. Second, little attention is devoted to developing and discussing a complete and coherent results chain linking diagnostics of gender issues to actions and activities and to indicators measuring the impact of those actions on gender inequalities and biases. This problem is especially visible in country strategies that integrate gender as a cross-cutting theme. Third, the indicators used in both projects and country strategy are often insufficient in capturing impacts on gender gaps, either because they are measuring outputs rather than outcomes, or are not sex-disaggregated, or are not formulated as well-defined and measurable indicators. Moreover, they are not always measured and reported.

It is important to recognize that many challenges the World Bank Group faces in integrating gender in its work are similar to and affected by broader systemic challenges frequently highlighted by IEG, such as deficits in articulating results chains and in M&E at both country and project levels. These general weaknesses contribute to many of the findings discussed in this chapter, and they need to be considered to fully appreciate the challenges in improving the approach to gender integration in the World Bank Group. It also needs to be acknowledged that project documents and country strategies on which the current analysis is based may neglect to report results that are actually achieved on the ground. So, one implication of the current analysis is that, for learning to occur on how to close gender gaps, the documentation of results in formal World Bank Group reporting documents has to improve.

The introduction of the first World Bank Group (joint IBRD–IFC) gender strategy in FY16 offers an opportunity to ensure that the mechanisms established to support gender integration in country strategies and projects are adjusted to generate and produce meaningful information and reporting. IEG's analysis shows this will not be achieved if the translation from policy to practice is marked by disconnected steps and requirements. Experience shows that meaningful engagement in gender integration is not simply a function of mechanical observance, but requires a multistep approach involving clear definition of the relevance of gender integration in the project or country strategy, discussion of the transmission channels generating impacts, identification of appropriate indicators to measure those impacts, and tracking, reporting, and evaluating results.

ENDNOTES

[1] Update on the Implementation of the Gender Equality Agenda at the World Bank Group, October 2014. Projects with gender in at least one dimension are 95 percent; in two dimensions 82 percent; and in three dimensions 55 percent. The Gender Unit in the Poverty Reduction and Economic Management network led the World Bank gender strategy until the 2014 restructuring, when the Gender Cross-Cutting Solution Area replaced it.

[2] "World Bank Group Corporate Scorecards" (September 24, 2015, presentation).

[3] IFC introduced the IFC gender flag in 2009/2010 for Advisory Services. This flag was revised in 2013 to match the World Bank approach; it was developed to capture multiple dimensions rather than a yes/no binary variable. In May 2015 the gender flag was introduced for Investment Services.

[4] Twenty-three in-depth interviews with select World Bank staff (representing different Regions and sectors, and mostly knowledgeable of the Bank strategy on gender) were conducted and formed the basis of a background paper to the MAR 2013.

[5] Of the 190 self-evaluated Advisory Services projects, 184 had been validated by IEG as of September 30, 2015.

[6] IEG reviewed all IFC projects that were self-evaluated by September 30, 2015, for the gender analysis.

[7] The Committee on Development Effectiveness discussed the concept note for the forthcoming gender strategy on April 8, 2015. A draft of the strategy was reviewed at vice-presidential level on September 28, 2015. The World Bank Group Board discussed the strategy document in December 2015.

[8] See http://siteresources.worldbank.org/INTGENDER/Resources/GenderFlag-GuidanceNote.pdf.

[9] This excludes from the 50 country strategies a few that only superficially mention gender (for example, country strategies that only include a few words, such as "the strategy will pay attention to gender issues").

[10] According to the indicator's definition in the Gender Scorecard, gender-integrated country strategies are those that integrate gender into: (a) analysis and/or consultation on gender-related issues; (b) specific actions to address the distinct needs of women and girls, or men and boys, and/or positive impacts on gender gaps; and (c) mechanisms to monitor gender impact, as explained at http://www-wds.worldbank.org/external/default/WDSContentServer/WDSP/IB/2014/10/09/000456286_20141009104938/Rendered/PDF/913110WP0World00Box385295B00PUBLIC0.pdf, page 24.

[11] In reporting that 95–97 percent of all projects were gender informed (based on the previous, looser criteria of gender being integrated in at least one dimension), the past gender updates of the gender mainstreaming strategy implicitly suggested that gender integration was expected of virtually all projects.

[12] IEG assessed relevance based on the project development objective (PDO) and the social impacts stated in the Project Appraisal Document, regardless of whether the project did or did not integrate any gender elements. The assessment also analyzed project components when needed. Considerable care was taken to define relevance (each project was reviewed and discussed by four team members), but important information on the context, the state of the policy dialogue, and other crucial elements are not fully reflected in project documents.

[13] Some categories are not mutually exclusive because boundaries are sometimes blurred (a project that misses the opportunity to address gaps may inadvertently amplify them).

[14] The analysis counted only projects with concrete gender actions.

[15] IEG recently adopted a strategic plan to improve the integration of gender in its evaluation work. The main objective of this plan is to identify viable approaches to systematically integrating gender in evaluation of strategies and operations so that gender-relevant results can be assessed and documented.

[16] The Twin Goals of the World Bank Group—reducing poverty and boosting shared prosperity—offer a good entry point for the integration of cross-cutting and overarching themes, including attention to gender.

[17] http://www.goldmansachs.com/citizenship/10000women/news-and-events/10000women-ifc.html.

[18] Seventy-seven (41 percent) of the 190 Advisory Services projects analyzed were joint Advisory Services–Investment Services projects.

[19] It may also be that embedding gender into a more broad and ambitious micro, small, and medium-sized enterprise banking project was perceived as too much for financial institution client subsidiaries to take on all at once.

[20] The Sustainability Framework consists of the Policy on Environmental and Social Sustainability, which defines IFC's commitments to environmental and social sustainability; the Performance Standards, which define clients' responsibilities for managing their environmental and social risks; the Access to Information Policy, which articulates IFC's commitment to transparency; and Environmental and Social Categorization. http://www.ifc.org/wps/wcm/connect/Topics_Ext_Content /IFC_External_Corporate_site/Sustainability+and+Disclosure/Environmental-Social-Governance/Sustainability +Framework.

[21] **Performance Standard 1** applies to all projects that trigger preparation of Stakeholder Engagement Plans because they have environmental and social risks and impacts, and are thus required to prepare an Environmental and Social Impact Assessment. The Performance Standards guidance note indicates that "gender-differentiated impacts should be assessed and the risks and impacts identification process should propose measures designed to ensure that one gender is not disadvantaged relative to the other in the context of the project. This may include providing opportunities to enhance full participation and influence in decision-making through separate mechanisms for consultation and grievances, and developing measures that allow both women and men equal access to benefits (such as land titles, compensation, and employment)." (IFC 2012b, p. 17.)

[22] In the Pakistan country strategy, the World Bank proposed technical assistance for the development of long-term exit and graduation-from-poverty strategies through targeted skills training and employment opportunities, especially for young people and women.

[23] IEG evaluations identified these weaknesses in the indicators used as part of monitoring and evaluation frameworks for World Bank Group projects and country strategies more generally, but that does not lessen the importance of developing appropriate indicators to meaningfully capture gender results.

[24] Results Frameworks in Country Strategies—Lessons from Evaluations (p.1). https://openknowledge.worldbank.org /handle/10986/21778.

[25] As with gender relevance, there are no guidelines defining a gender indicator. Although person-level indicators disaggregated by sex allow an easy comparison of outcomes for males and females, women-specific indicators are more problematic, and for some it may be questioned whether they are "gender indicators" at all—that is, presumably,

useful in monitoring gender equality and biases. For example, provision of prenatal care, antiretroviral treatment for pregnant patients, or skilled birth attendance may be considered health indicators rather than gender indicators because they do not measure whether these activities were performed in a gender-sensitive way.

[26] PDO-level gender indicators means those that were reported at sex-disaggregated level or were male- or female-specific.

[27] The ICR reporting on the gender impacts of the project discussed the benefits of increased poor women's participation in rural road maintenance and its impact on women's economic empowerment. The project M&E was able to capture gender disaggregated impacts of involving women in routine rural roads maintenance, despite the absence of indicators at design stage. The ICR did a good job showcasing these results. The ICR Review highlights a lesson specific to the results on gender: "Gender-based community-driven small-scale road maintenance can be an effective way to tackle local road maintenance issues. The Women's Union supported under the project to manage the routine communal road maintenance proved to be cost effective. Contractors were not interested in small contracts for the type of routine work that the Women's Union was carrying out on communal roads. The ICR (p. 24) finds that the gender-based community-driven small-scale road maintenance also raised awareness, built a sense of local ownership, fostered local stewardship of local roads, and changed behavior to protect rather than damage roads."

[28] The female beneficiaries indicator was added in half of the instances where PDO gender indicators were added during implementation.

[29] Core sector indicators are indicators (outcome and output) measured and monitored at the project level that can be aggregated across projects and countries for corporate reporting. Corporate indicators are available for 26 sectors and themes across the World Bank and their use is mandatory for IBRD and IDA operations. http://intranet.worldbank.org/WBSITE/INTRANET/UNITS/INTOPICS/0,,menuPK:6250526~contentMDK:22226896~menuPK:6250526~pagePK:51455324~piPK:3763353~theSitePK:380832,00.html.

[30] This analysis could not determine whether producing sex-disaggregated indicators was possible in practice or whether there were cost implications. IEG could not find an example of project documents that justified the absence of sex-disaggregated indicators.

[31] The ICR had done a good job reporting on sex-disaggregated results and also discussing qualitatively the project's impacts on women's economic and social empowerment. The ICR notes: "According to the beneficiary survey conducted, beneficiaries of project activities perceived significant changes in gender-related issues. The situation of women has considerably improved due to water and health infrastructures built, as well as associated sensitization programs in hygiene and family planning. In addition, the support for revenue-generating activities has given women beneficiaries more opportunities to some financial autonomy. At the same time, the implementation of the program has opened the way for women to integrate village associations as equal partners like men and so to share the decision-making process at the community level. Project activities have also had positive effects on intercommunities and intergenerational relationships. These consist of peaceful conflict management between social groups with different interests and the promotion of youth involvement in decision making process, both contributing to more social equity and inclusion. The project has contributed significantly to the empowerment of women by (i) reducing the burden of chores with access to facilities, equipment, food processing in particular, and (ii) significantly increasing their employment, income and thus their participation in family expenses. In fact, a large proportion of productive projects funded under PACR (about 40%) benefited to women whose OSP constituted the vast majority (over 80%) of those who have succeeded in some areas. Finally, through PACR, women did benefit of better access to health related services through health centers. PACR interventions have introduced significant changes for the major players in grassroots development through improving:...(ii) income levels of rural producers and especially women producers who became more independent; and assisted deliveries (around 97.5% of women gave birth at centers supported by PACR and the remaining 2.5% gave birth with the assistance of an health agent;.... Moreover, these organizations have created more than 77,000 jobs, including 38,400 jobs for women."

[32] Not all indicators are collected for all clients. For example, the employment indicator is not collected for financial institutions.

[33] In 2014 almost 100 percent of IFC's active clients reported information on female employment. Although the

data cannot be used to attribute jobs to IFC projects, it may provide signaling, which could allow IFC to focus its work, strategy, and incentives on those areas with the most potential or promise. For example, data show that Manufacturing, Agribusiness, and Services clients have the most employees, of which 35 percent are female. IFC does not require financial markets clients to report employment data because of the difficulty in collecting this information from sub-borrowers.

REFERENCES

Independent Evaluation Group (IEG). 2010. *Gender and Development: An Evaluation of World Bank Support 2002–08.* Washington, DC: World Bank.

———. 2013a. "Biennial Report on Operations Evaluation (BROE): Assessing the Monitoring and Evaluation Systems of IFC and MIGA." IEG Approach Paper No. 72691, World Bank, Washington, DC.

———. 2013b. *Youth Employment Programs: An Evaluation of World Bank and International Finance Corporation Support.* Washington, DC: World Bank.

———. 2014. *Social Safety Nets and Gender: Learning from Impact Evaluations and World Bank Projects.* Washington, DC: World Bank.

———. 2015a. *Financial Inclusion—A Foothold on the Ladder toward Prosperity? An Evaluation of World Bank Group Support for Financial Inclusion for Low-Income Households and Microenterprises.* Washington, DC: World Bank.

———. 2015b. *Investment Climate Reforms: An Independent Evaluation of World Bank Group Support to Reforms of Business Regulations.* Washington, DC: World Bank.

———. 2015c. *The Poverty Focus of Country Programs: Lessons from World Bank Experience.* Washington, DC: World Bank.

———. 2015d. *World Bank Group Engagement in Resource-Rich Developing Countries: The Cases of the Plurinational State of Bolivia, Kazakhstan, Mongolia, and Zambia.* Washington, DC: World Bank.

———. 2015e. *World Bank Group Support to Electricity Access, FY2000–FY2014: An Independent Evaluation.* Washington, DC: World Bank.

International Finance Corporation (IFC). 2012a. *IFC Sustainability Framework: Policy and Performance Standards on Environmental and Social Sustainability, Access to Information Policy.* Washington, DC: IFC. http://www .ifc.org/wps/wcm/ connect/b9dacb004a73e7a8a273fff998895a12/ IFC_Sustainability_+Framework .pdf?MOD=AJPERES.

———. 2012b. "Performance Standards on Environmental and Social Sustainability." January 1, 2012. Washington, DC: IFC. http://www.ifc.org/wps/wcm/connect/ 115482804a0255db96 fbffd1a5d13d27 /PS_English_2012_Full-Document.pdf?MOD=AJPERES.

———. 2013. "IFC Road Map FY14-16: Leveraging the Private Sector to Eradicate Extreme Poverty and Pursue Shared Prosperity." Washington, DC: IFC.

———. 2014. "IFC Road Map FY15-17: Implementing the World Bank Group Strategy." Washington, DC: IFC.

Mollard, Ingrid, Emily Brearley, Marialena Vyzaki, and Sanna-Liisa Taivalmaa. 2015. "Beyond Quality at Entry: Portfolio Review on Gender Implementation of Agriculture Projects (FY08–13)." Agricultural Global Practice Technical Assistance Paper No. 94753, World Bank, Washington, DC.

World Bank. 2002. *Integrating Gender into the World Bank's Work: A Strategy for Action.* Washington, DC: World Bank.

———. 2006. *Gender Equality as Smart Economics: A World Bank Group Gender Action Plan (Fiscal years 2007–10).* Washington, DC: World Bank.

———. 2012. "Update on the Implementation of the Gender Equality Agenda at the World Bank Group." DC2014-0010. Washington, DC: World Bank.

———. 2015. *World Bank Group Gender Strategy (FY16-23): Gender Equality, Poverty Reduction, and Inclusive Growth.* Washington, DC: World Bank.

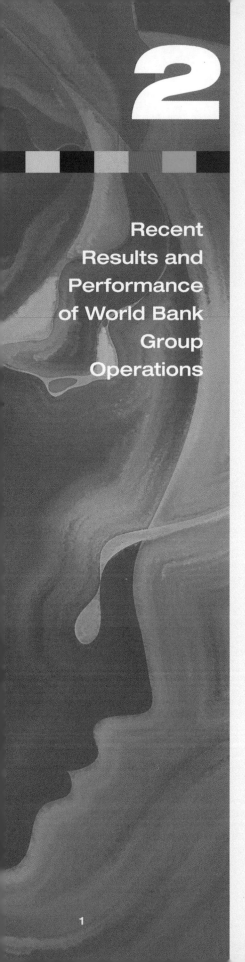

2

Recent Results and Performance of World Bank Group Operations

highlights

1 The performance of World Bank projects completed during FY12–14, measured by commitment, already exceeded FY17 corporate targets; measured by number, overall project performance holds steady, but below the FY17 corporate target

2 International Finance Corporation (IFC) Advisory Services and Multilateral Investment Guarantee (MIGA) guarantee projects continue to perform in line with previous years, but the downward trend for IFC investment projects, reported since 2013, continues

3 Initial commitment size is not a key element of success for World Bank projects, but the change in commitments during a project (such as cancellation or additional financing) significantly correlated with project outcome rating

4 Quality at entry and supervision continue to be the key factors explaining project outcomes

5 Size matters for IFC real sector projects, but not to the same extent as other risk factors (for example, management quality, market conditions, investment climate, and work quality).

World Bank Group commitments rise after the postfinancial crisis decline

WORLD BANK GROUP COMMITMENTS rose for two consecutive years and reached $60 billion in FY15 (Figure 2.1).[1]

International Bank for Reconstruction and Development (IBRD) lending increased from $19 billion in FY14 to $24 billion in FY15, while International Development Association (IDA) commitments fell from an all-time high of $22 billion in FY14 to $19 billion in FY15. Investment project financing increased from $28.6 billion in FY14 to $30.5 billion in FY15. During the same period, commitments for development policy financing declined from $10.5 billion to $9.2 billion, and commitments for the relatively new Program for Results instrument introduced in FY12 continued a steady increase from $1.7 billion in FY14 and to $2.2 billion in FY15.[2]

In FY15 the World Bank Group organized its Global Practices (GPs) into three clusters. Commitments were greatest for the Sustainable Development cluster at $22 billion (52 percent of total commitments), followed by the Economic Growth, Finance, and Institutions cluster at $11 billion, and the Human Development cluster at $9.3 billion.

The Bank provides advisory services and analytics (ASA) support to clients as freestanding services or as a complement to lending programs. In FY14 the Bank delivered 981 ASA products amounting to $248 million.

IFC long-term commitments ($10.5 billion) were up about 6 percent over the previous year. The largest increase was in the Financial Institutions Group (about 45 percent of total commitments), which increased most in the East Asia and Pacific Region, where IFC supported a large Indonesian Bank to help it better serve microenterprises. Commitments fell sharply in the Europe and Central Asia Region, where ongoing regional tensions and economic contraction affected business volumes. IFC long-term commitments and net income fell sharply in FY16 first-quarter commitments compared with the same quarter in FY15 (IEG 2015). IFC's report attributes changes in net income and portfolio performance partly to "a number of factors," including volatile equity markets, currency depreciation, lower commodity prices, and some adverse project-specific developments. This report highlights other factors that affected performance, including a continued downward trend in IFC work quality.

IFC, in addition to commitments for its own account, mobilizes funds from other institutions. IFC's core mobilization increased in FY15 by about $2 billion to $7.1 billion, driven mostly by syndicated loans. Asset Management Company (IFC's fund management business) share of core mobilization remained modest at 11 percent. IEG has not independently evaluated Asset Management Company's operations; IFC's average outstanding balance of short-term finance declined over the same period.[3] IFC restructured its Advisory Services operations in FY14. IFC expenditure on advisory work in FY15 decreased 15 percent (to $202 million) compared with a year earlier, and the number of active advisory projects fell from 719 to 600. The proportion of all IFC advisory work undertaken in IDA and fragile or conflict-affected situations (65 percent) remained unchanged.

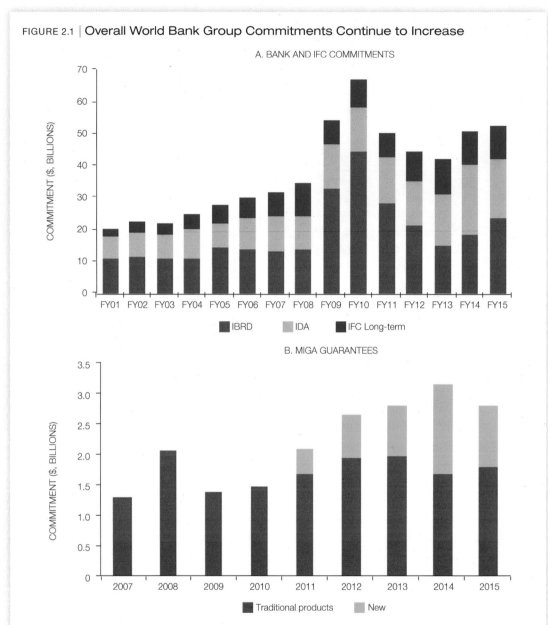

FIGURE 2.1 | Overall World Bank Group Commitments Continue to Increase

A. BANK AND IFC COMMITMENTS

IBRD   IDA   IFC Long-term

B. MIGA GUARANTEES

Traditional products   New

Sources: World Bank Business Intelligence; IFC and MIGA databases.

Note: Commitments for IFC exclude mobilization. In FY15 IFC began reporting average outstanding short-term commitments (not total commitments) and no longer aggregates short-term commitments with long-term commitments.

MIGA issued 40 guarantees for $2.8 billion in FY15 compared with 24 guarantees for $3.2 billion in FY14, when MIGA supported two large guarantees of $500 million and more. Guarantees in FY15 included six for non-honoring of financial obligations[4] that, in addition to financial sector projects, supported transportation projects, which helped MIGA diversify its business; before FY10, it was dominated by banking and financial services projects.

World Bank project performance stabilizes

After a declining trend, the overall performance of World Bank projects with project outcomes rated as moderately satisfactory and above (MS+) stabilized at 70 percent, but was below the corporate target of 75 percent by FY17 (based on 93 percent of IEG's FY14 validation).[5] However, when weighting the percentage of MS+ projects by net commitment,[6] Bank projects' performance exceeded the FY17 corporate target of 80 percent, with a success rate of 81 percent for the period FY12–14.[7]

Performance of IPF projects—the largest instrument type in number and commitment—mirrored overall World Bank performance during FY12–14 at 69 percent. About 78 percent of development policy financing (DPF) projects had MS+ outcome ratings (Figure 2.2). It is notable that policy-based loans

FIGURE 2.2 | **Projects Rated Moderately Satisfactory or Above by IEG**

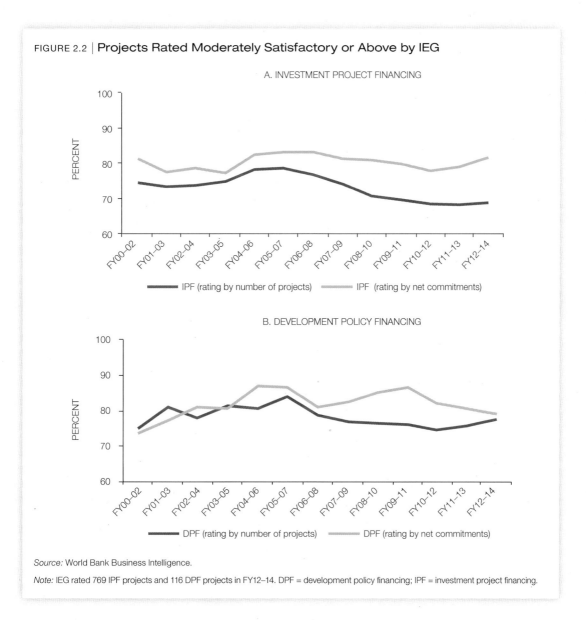

Source: World Bank Business Intelligence.

Note: IEG rated 769 IPF projects and 116 DPF projects in FY12–14. DPF = development policy financing; IPF = investment project financing.

Box 2.1 | Recent Performance Trends of Development Policy Financing Projects

According to IEG's review, within the group of moderately satisfactory and above (MS+) projects, there has been a shift toward the "moderate" side of satisfactory—that is, the proportion of operations with moderately satisfactory outcome rating has increased, and the proportion of satisfactory projects has decreased. The growing share of moderately satisfactory projects in development policy financing is driven by an increase in the share of develoment policy financing (DPF) projects with weak design (rated "modest" or below). The proportion of operations with weak design was 33 percent in 2009–11; in 2012–14 it was 44 percent. But this increase is not necessarily an indication of weakening quality— other factors, such as streamlining of self-evaluation, validation, and evaluation standards might have also contributed to the trend.

Evaluative evidence from IEG's project-level validation and evaluation suggests that several key factors affect design quality in DPF projects. These include weaknesses in the results chain underpinning the programs (owing to poor links between policy actions and expected outcomes), weak relevance of policy actions supported by DPF projects to the stated objectives, and mismatch between choice of the instrument and the reforms' ambitions (mostly in cases of stand-alone operations with a short time horizon).

---

are inherently different from investment lending projects,[8] and comparing the two is not necessarily meaningful. Furthermore, it is inappropriate to compare rating achievements across instruments because of differences in assessment methodologies.[9] DPF performance, measured by the percentage of projects rated MS+, improved during FY09–15 (Box 2.1);[10] however, when weighted by net commitment, there is a slight decline caused by some large operations rated moderately unsatisfactory or below (MS−).

Performance of Bank projects was strongest in the South Asia Region, declined in the East Asia and Pacific Region, and was lowest in the Middle East and North Africa Region
World Bank project performance in IDA countries improved from 68 percent in FY09–11 to 73 percent FY12–14,[11] but performance in fragile and conflict-affected situations remained unchanged at about 68 percent. MS+ ratings for projects in IBRD countries declined from 73 percent to 66 percent in the same period, which is statistically significant (Figure 2.3). (Unless otherwise noted, statistical significance of comparisons in this chapter is at the 10 percent level.)

At the regional level, the World Bank performance was strongest in the South Asia Region (79 percent MS+). The East Asia and Pacific Region showed the sharpest decline, from 75 percent to 65 percent MS+ between FY09–11 and FY12–14 (statistically significant at the 10 percent level). Although slightly improved from FY09–11, performance in the Middle East and North Africa Region (64 percent MS+) is the lowest among all Regions (Figure 2.4). IEG's Region Updates provide more information based on Project Performance Assessment Reports (see Appendix E).

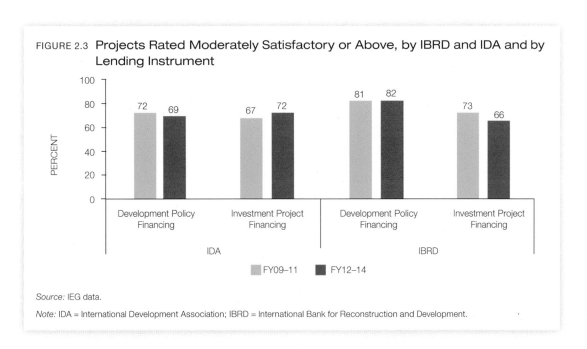

FIGURE 2.3 Projects Rated Moderately Satisfactory or Above, by IBRD and IDA and by Lending Instrument

Source: IEG data.

Note: IDA = International Development Association; IBRD = International Bank for Reconstruction and Development.

The performance decline in East Asia and Pacific Region was partly due to a drop in well-performing projects in IBRD countries (67 percent of evaluated projects) and blend countries (18 percent of evaluated projects) from 72 percent to 58 percent and 86 percent to 68 percent, respectively. Project performance in three countries—accounting for 50 percent of evaluated projects—drove this decline. The project performance rate declined from 91 percent to 73 percent in China and from 86 percent to 77 percent in Vietnam. The already low performance of projects in the Philippines further deteriorated from 38 percent to 23 percent, and Indonesia's low performance remained at 58 percent and 59 percent.

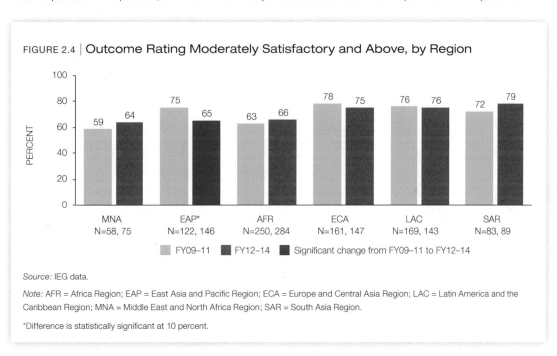

FIGURE 2.4 | Outcome Rating Moderately Satisfactory and Above, by Region

Source: IEG data.

Note: AFR = Africa Region; EAP = East Asia and Pacific Region; ECA = Europe and Central Asia Region; LAC = Latin America and the Caribbean Region; MNA = Middle East and North Africa Region; SAR = South Asia Region.

*Difference is statistically significant at 10 percent.

Performance was particularly strong in the Social Protection and Labor, and Agriculture Global Practices

Performance by GPs has been assessed based on the mapping of the projects which was conducted bank-wide in 2014 when the Global Practices were instituted. The Social Protection and Labor GP performed the best out of the 14 GPs, with 91 percent of 32 projects rated MS+ during FY12–14 compared with 74 percent of 38 projects rated MS+ during FY09–11 (which is statistically significant at the 10 percent level). Portfolio reviews and interviews with sector specialists indicate that four factors help explain this strong performance. First, many Social Protection and Labor GP projects are strongly evidence-based and have relatively high ratings for quality at entry (76 percent of projects rated MS+), which is a key correlate for positive project outcome. Second, supervision quality is also highly rated, with 89 percent of projects rated MS+. Third, evaluation is often built into project design, which led to steady improvement in the monitoring and evaluation (M&E) frameworks for relevant projects (59 percent are rated substantial or better on M&E in FY12–14 compared with 41 percent between FY09–11 and with an overall Bank average of 30 percent). Fourth, IEG found that among GPs, Social Protection and Labor produced the third largest share (7 percent) of impact evaluations (according to an IEG follow-up analysis on its 2012 evaluation of the relevance of World Bank Group impact evaluations). IEG found the Social Protection and Labor GP effectively implemented recommendations from IEG's evaluation of social safety nets (IEG 2011), including increasing support to strengthen institutional capacity.

Project performance in the Agriculture GP also improved significantly during the two periods, from 51 percent to 74 percent (statistically significant at the 5 percent level). The mix or typology of projects did not change noticeably during this period. A document review assessed whether project development objectives (PDOs) fell into one of two categories: clear-cut and straightforward, or multifaceted and long-duration,[12] and found an increase in the share of clear-cut and straightforward PDOs in FY12–14 (44 percent to 61 percent). Challenging land and forestry reform projects, as well as environment-focused projects in watershed and sustainable land management, performed at similarly poor levels during both periods, though community-driven development projects and those responding to the global food crisis performed exceptionally well during both periods.

Decline in performance was observed for the Environment and Natural Resources GP

Among the 14 GPs, the Environment and Natural Resources GP showed the only statistically significant decline in performance between FY09–11 and FY12–14: performance fell from 69 percent to 51 percent MS+ for 58 projects evaluated in FY09–11 and 55 in FY12–14. Within this portfolio, IDA projects rated MS+ dropped by 35 percent, Global Environment Facility (GEF) projects dropped by 21 percent, and IBRD projects by 10 percent.[13] GEF projects seemed to be the largest contributor to the poor performance because of their large number, which is about four to six times the number of IBRD and IDA projects. By Region, Sub-Saharan Africa was the worst performer in the Environment and Natural Resources GP, where no GEF projects were rated MS+ during FY12–14 compared with 60 percent during FY09–11 (Figure 2.5). IEG reviewed the Implementation Completion and Results Reviews (ICRRs) for GEF projects rated moderately unsatisfactory or below and found three key reasons for low ratings: (a) negligible or modest achievements of outputs and outcomes; (b) little or no evidence to support claimed results, usually accompanied by poor M&E; and (c) negligible or modest efficiency due to serious administrative inefficiencies and long delays, low rates of return, or wrong calculation methodology for economic rate of return.

Development policy financing is concentrated in three GPs: Governance, Macroeconomics and Fiscal Management, and Finance and Markets. It showed no significant change in performance over time.[14]

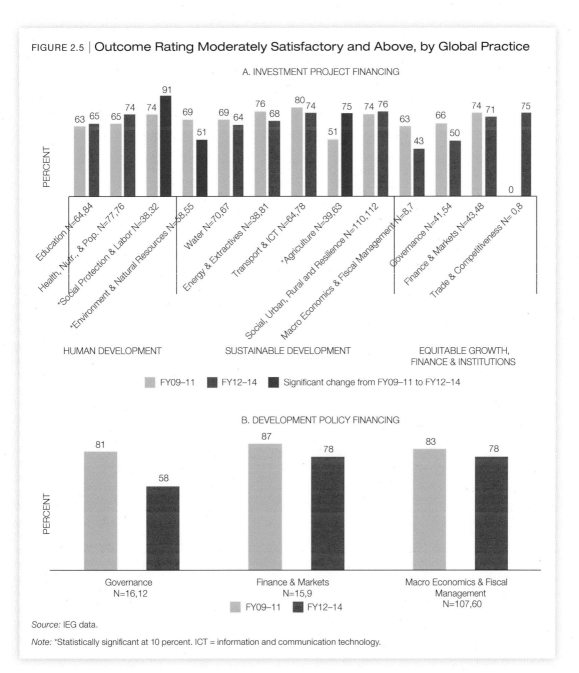

FIGURE 2.5 | Outcome Rating Moderately Satisfactory and Above, by Global Practice

Source: IEG data.

Note: *Statistically significant at 10 percent. ICT = information and communication technology.

However, at 58 percent MS+, the Governance GP—for which 12 projects were rated during FY12–14—was the lowest performer.

Development outcomes for IFC investment projects continue to decline

The downward trend reported by IEG in development outcome ratings for IFC-supported investment projects since 2013 continues. Fifty-eight percent of the 225 mature investment operations evaluated in 2012–14[15] had development outcome ratings of mostly successful or higher compared with 68 percent of projects evaluated in 2009–11 (Figure 2.6).[16] Projects that fail to achieve a mostly successful rating tend to fall short of IFC's established financial, economic, environmental, and social performance benchmarks, and do not contribute more broadly to private sector development in the local economies in which they operate (Box 2.2).[17]

Falling equity success rates moved investment success rates lower, continuing a trend that began in 2009–11. Equity investments are inherently riskier than loans, and IFC should expect lower equity success rates, but higher overall equity returns to compensate for the added risk. Recent equity success rates of 23 percent are lower than the historical rate of 35 percent. The current low success level is partly owing to negative effects from the global financial currency devaluations reduced equity values in dollar terms; funds were slower to invest; manufacturers saw product demand fall; and weakened management and sponsors found it difficult to cope. Puts, or convertible equity, was in many cases insufficient to remedy low equity valuations. In 2015 IFC's net income suffered from relatively low realized equity returns.

IFC operations in non-IDA countries saw a significant, steep decline in performance since CY07–09, while operations in IDA and blend countries improved during the last two reporting periods. Statistically significant declines in investment outcomes and work quality were also observed in non-IDA countries. All development sub-indicators, except for environmental and social effects and project supervision, were also down significantly. In IDA and blend countries, IEG observed improving private sector development ratings and role and contribution. A closer look at the portfolio shows that recently evaluated projects in manufacturing and services performed poorly, as did projects in the Europe and Central Asia and East Asia and Pacific Regions (Figure 2.7).

Performance dropped significantly in the Europe and Central Asia and East Asia and Pacific Regions. The performance decline in Europe and Central Asia was partly associated with low ratings for evaluated projects in Ukraine. In East Asia and the Pacific, most of the projects evaluated in China during the CY12–14 period (manufacturing and technology sector projects most severely affected by the downturn) were rated low. IFC also supported seven regional projects—five in Europe and Central Asia and two in East Asia and the Pacific. Five of the seven projects invested in funds, none of which were rated successful or better for development. All rated low for work quality, and only one project provided IFC with a return commensurate with risk. Overall, funds performed worse than the portfolio of evaluated projects. Reasons for the decline include misaligned incentives, difficulties in

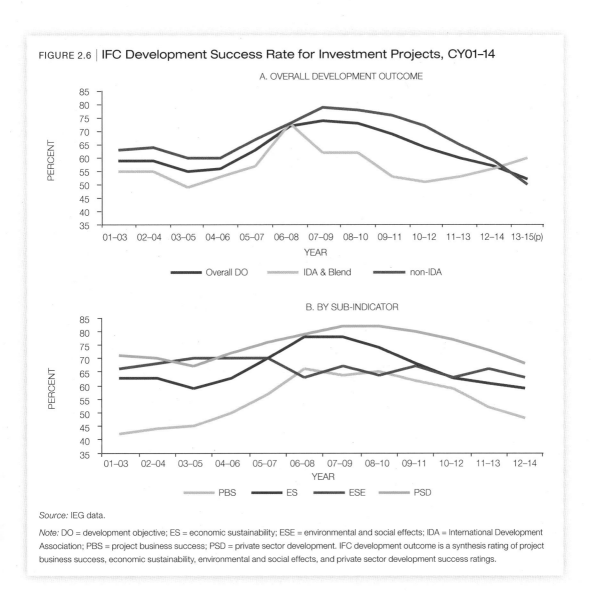

FIGURE 2.6 | IFC Development Success Rate for Investment Projects, CY01–14

A. OVERALL DEVELOPMENT OUTCOME

Overall DO — IDA & Blend — non-IDA

B. BY SUB-INDICATOR

PBS — ES — ESE — PSD

Source: IEG data.

Note: DO = development objective; ES = economic sustainability; ESE = environmental and social effects; IDA = International Development Association; PBS = project business success; PSD = private sector development. IFC development outcome is a synthesis rating of project business success, economic sustainability, environmental and social effects, and private sector development success ratings.

exiting funds during tough economic times, standardized approaches across Regions to assess and structure IFC investments in funds, and mismatched expertise in IFC industry team–originated funds (versus IFC funds teams).

Project performance in the IFC industry group was relatively stable except in manufacturing, agribusiness, and services, where a significant decline was recorded. A review of relevant projects shows that the global financial crisis affected some projects, making it more difficult to secure funding or attract customers (tourism projects, for example). IFC project evaluations also noted other problems that affected recent services projects, including a lack of commitment, expertise, or implementation discipline among sponsors, and poor IFC work quality. A number of innovative or greenfield projects also failed (Figure 2.8).

Box 2.2 | Evaluation of Investment Projects at IFC

IFC evaluates projects based on three dimensions and nine indicators that together address a project's contribution to IFC's purpose and mission, the impact of the investment on IFC's financial sustainability, and IFC's work quality. Evaluations measure development outcome across four indicators: project business success, economic sustainability, environmental and social effects, and private sector development success ratings (Figure 2.6). IFC's investment outcome assesses the extent to which IFC is likely to realize the loan or equity returns expected at approval. Work quality addresses IFC's screening, appraisal, and structuring; supervision and administration; and role and contribution. A stratified random sample of IFC projects that have reached early operating maturity is evaluated.

IFC work quality continues to need attention; though it showed some minor but statistically insignificant improvement in year-on-year results (comparing CY13 with CY14), overall work quality ratings continued their decline to 67 percent. *Results and Performance of the World Bank Group 2014* (IEG 2014b) analyzed work quality components such as risk identification and mitigation as strong contributors to screening, appraisal, and structuring (up-front work quality) ratings—a strong driver of project success. A decline in the quality of Expanded Project Supervision Reports (XPSRs), or self-evaluation documents, was consistent with the decline in work quality. Measured as a proportion of all XPSRs, more than 40 percent were considered good practice between 2001 and 2007 compared with fewer than 25 percent in recent years. The quality of lessons written in XPSRs varied.[18]

FIGURE 2.7 | IFC Development Performance, by Region

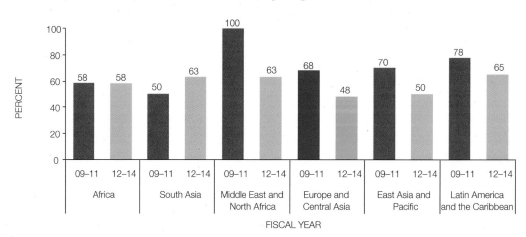

Source: IEG data.

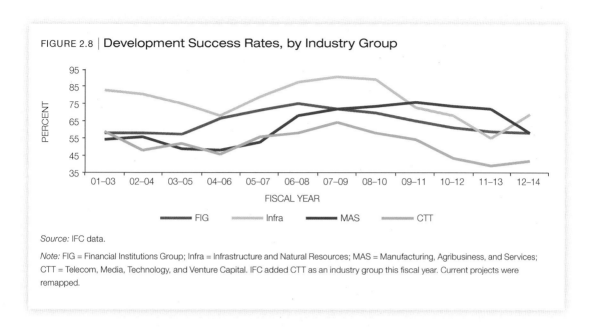

FIGURE 2.8 | Development Success Rates, by Industry Group

PERCENT

FISCAL YEAR

━━━ FIG   ⋯⋯⋯ Infra   ━━━ MAS   ━━━ CTT

Source: IFC data.

Note: FIG = Financial Institutions Group; Infra = Infrastructure and Natural Resources; MAS = Manufacturing, Agribusiness, and Services; CTT = Telecom, Media, Technology, and Venture Capital. IFC added CTT as an industry group this fiscal year. Current projects were remapped.

IFC additionality (IFC's benefit or value addition that a client would not otherwise receive) is the main justification for IFC involvement in a project. Through its additionality IFC can strengthen a project by, for instance, mitigating risks or improving a client's capacity, and ultimately improving a project's chances to succeed and enhance its development impact. IEG found better development results when additionality was present, and that there was no clear trade-off between additionality and IFC's profitability.

IFC achieved higher development impact when it delivered combinations of funding and knowledge-based additionality together, particularly to high-risk projects (for example, in IDA countries and for high-risk sponsors). However, delivering such combinations of funding and knowledge-based additionality is more challenging compared to funding or knowledge-based additionality alone. This is owing mainly to the difficulty of delivering knowledge-based additionality, which depends heavily on IFC's ability to deploy support to the client or project over the length of the entire project life cycle. IEG has also found that there is scope to enhance the use of additionality to position IFC strategically in different country and client contexts.

IFC's additionality is an integral part of IFC's overall role and contribution, which is assessed under the work quality dimension.

There has been a decline in IFC's role and contribution success rates since 2008. A qualitative review of the evaluated portfolio suggests that role and contribution fares better when IFC sets realistic expectations at approval by focusing on the additionalities it can best deliver; gathers resources needed to realize such additionalities; and ensures that client understanding, readiness, and commitment are present. Overall, IEG found that role and contribution ranked second to front-end work quality in contributing to development outcome.

IFC integrated client-facing Advisory and Investment Services after reorganizing in 2014, with the goal of sharpening additionality and enhancing overall development impact. Almost all of the CY12–14

Access to Finance private sector projects to build client capacity had links to IFC financial clients in some form, and half of all Sustainable Business Advisory projects had links to IFC investments.

IFC's Advisory Services' performance was steady. IEG found that IFC's Advisory Services performed well, with overall development effectiveness reaching 63 percent for FY12–14 compared with 58 percent for CY09–11 (Figure 2.9). IEG also found that Advisory Services benefitted IFC's financial sector clients. They enhanced development results by engaging with IFC investment clients in the financial sector, achieving a 70 percent development success rate. Government-facing engagements achieved success rates comparable to those of private client-facing projects (65 percent and 64 percent, respectively). Public-private partnership success rates were in line with the previous period, reflecting the high-risk nature of the business.

IFC's work quality on Advisory Services projects was a crucial driver of success, with project preparation and customization to client and local conditions key. Rolling out standard products and customizing them during project inception was often unsuccessful, especially in higher-risk projects. However, tailoring the project design using deep knowledge of the client and the local market improved the chances for success. Project scope was another factor that influenced project success. Advisory projects that were well and narrowly defined produced better results than wide-ranging projects. A measured, phased approach, coupled with a focus on priority areas, activities sequenced with client and market needs, and delivering advice to a single client, were often contributors to project success. Assessing client capacity early in the project was also important to achieving success, as was investment in building client capacity to address weaknesses.

Performance of MIGA guarantees are stable with some weaknesses

IEG rated 63 percent of the 56 MIGA guarantee projects evaluated in FY09–14 satisfactory or above for development outcome (Figure 2.10). Projects in the agribusiness, manufacturing, and services sectors had the highest success rate (75 percent), although the small number of evaluated agribusiness projects within this group performed poorly. The poor performance (50 percent) for financial markets projects

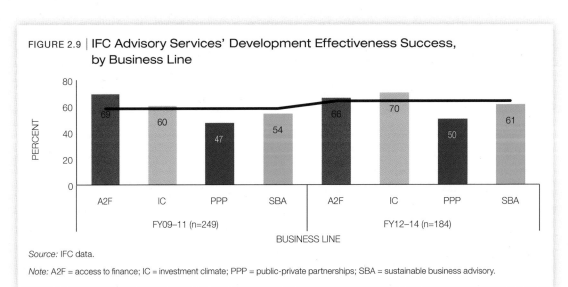

FIGURE 2.9 | **IFC Advisory Services' Development Effectiveness Success, by Business Line**

Source: IFC data.

Note: A2F = access to finance; IC = investment climate; PPP = public-private partnerships; SBA = sustainable business advisory.

(most of which are in the Europe and Central Asia Region), including generally low environmental and social effects ratings,[19] is a reversal of recently reported results. Projects were unsuccessful because of:

- Poor financial performance due to increased macroeconomic instability caused by the financial crisis and specific characteristics of the financial institutions;

- Loan portfolio contraction in some institutions instead of an expected expansion; and

- High leverage in some projects.

IEG conducted the first evaluation of an active non-honoring of financial obligations (NHFO) guarantee in FY15 and found that MIGA's NHFO products can play a valuable countercyclical role in helping fundamentally sound projects access financial markets during times of crisis. The evaluation also suggests that MIGA strengthen its monitoring systems for NHFO guarantees because these products directly take the credit risk of the sovereign, sub-sovereign, or state-owned enterprise (depending on the NHFO guarantee) and carry a higher risk level compared with traditional political risk insurance coverage.

For World Bank projects, some country and project factors matter more than initial size

This report intends to provide insight on recent World Bank results and performance. Questions of interest include how effective the projects were in delivering development results, key factors associated with performance, and lessons learned for incorporating into the design and implementation of future projects. Considering the Board discussions on the findings of RAP 2014 (IEG 2014b), this analysis looks at possible differences in performance of World Bank investment

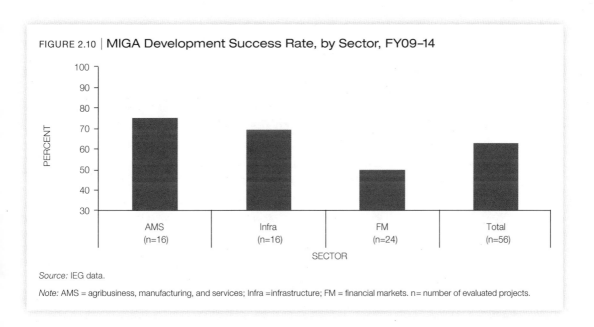

FIGURE 2.10 | MIGA Development Success Rate, by Sector, FY09–14

Source: IEG data.

Note: AMS = agribusiness, manufacturing, and services; Infra =infrastructure; FM = financial markets. n= number of evaluated projects.

lending projects based on the size of the project and other factors related to project and country context.[20]

In this report, as in previous years, the main measure of World Bank project results is the IEG-validated outcome rating from ICRRs, consisting of relevance, efficacy, and efficiency. IEG also validates other ratings in ICRs such as Bank performance (quality at entry and supervision) and borrower performance (government and implementing agencies), and rates the quality of the project's M&E.[21] The structure of this reporting and rating system enables logically sound comparison across projects. However, projects also have complexities that might not fit easily into the current reporting structures, including important contextual factors such as a country's economic situation, institutional capacity, and political economy considerations, among others. Indicators such as the World Governance Indicators, the Gender Inequality Index, and Country Policy and Institutional Assessment (CPIA), which is a measure of institutional capacity in the country, can shed some light on country context. Project performance also varies on factors internal to an operation, such as performance of the task team leader and team, or time and resources devoted to problem solving. This analysis does not explain success in projects, but rather looks at what can be learned from data such as the number of task team leaders assigned to a project and the project supervision cost.

Analysis of data on IPF projects[22] closed in FY09–14 finds that project performance is highly correlated with quality at entry, quality of supervision, M&E quality, and, to a much lesser extent, project size (see appendix B for correlations).[23] The discussion of project size arises in part from attention to the World Bank's Corporate Scorecard, which shows higher performance of larger projects because it reports on performance in two ways: a simple percentage of projects rated MS+, and a volume-weighted percentage.[24] Investigation beyond the Corporate Scorecard, however, shows that project size also correlates with a number of other factors. Project size positively correlates with ICRR ratings for quality at entry, quality of supervision, and quality of M&E; project restructuring; population of the country; CPIA; public opinion about the effectiveness of the World Bank's work in the country; government effectiveness; and rule of law ratings (from the World Governance Indicators). Project size negatively correlates with the country's fragile and conflict-affected situation (FCS) status, and gender equality as measured by the Gender Inequality Index (selected for use because of the theme of this report). Project size and project outcome ratings also vary across Regions and GPs.

IEG developed a regression model to look further into project size, and to understand the many other factors that also correlate with outcomes.[25] Two important elements—quality at entry and quality at supervision—were not included in the model because these ratings are assigned at the same time and by the same evaluator as the outcome rating (in the Implementation Completion and Results Review, after the project is completed). If quality at entry were systematically rated at appraisal or at the first Implementation Status and Results report, the rating would probably be extremely useful for predicting project performance. However, there is no systematic practice of assessing quality at entry early in World Bank projects, and therefore there are no data.

The model explained about 28 percent of the variation in outcome, and project size explained half of that (14 percent). There are two implications: first, that the additional variables explained about as much variation in outcome as did project size; second, that the current data do *not* explain more than two-thirds of the variation in outcome. A systematic measure of ex-ante quality at entry would likely help explain the missing two-thirds of the variation.

Within the 14 percent of variation explained by factors other than size in the current model, however, two factors related to country and project context merit discussing.

Country Capacity Matters

Country populations and CPIA ratings were significant among the country factors that helped explain performance, probably because large projects tend to have higher public sector management and institutional capacity, better social inclusion, and equity. Related analysis suggests that projects in countries with greater gender equality, more effective government functions, or more stable rule of law are also associated with higher outcome ratings.[26]

Larger country population was also associated with higher outcome ratings. However, outcome ratings for projects in India and China drove this association; population sizes in these countries make them outliers. When projects in India and China are excluded from the regression analysis using the same model, the coefficient is no longer significant. Without India and China, 89 percent of the World Bank IPF portfolio (by lending volume) was rated moderately satisfactory or above. Outcome ratings for projects in India and China are not statistically different from each other—by volume, the percentage of projects rated moderately satisfactory or above was 84 percent for India and 85 percent for China. The coefficients for other country factors used as control variables (gross domestic product per capita, fragile and conflict-affected status) were not significant.

Midcourse Corrections Can Enhance Outcomes of World Bank Projects

Among the project factors that helped explain outcomes, change in commitment was significant and positively correlated with outcome, while initial commitment was less significant. This comparison suggests that project performance relates more to what happens during project implementation— such as cancelling funds for projects that are not working or additional financing for successful projects—than to the initial commitment size of the project.

Although size and ratings correlate, improved performance associated with the difference in commitment amount at appraisal and at project closure may be owing to the practice of directing more resources to projects that are performing well during implementation and discontinuing those that are not.[27] Further analysis suggests that the correlation between cancellation of funds and low outcome ratings is stronger than the correlation between additional financing and high outcome ratings. Figure 2.11 plots the pattern in outcome ratings by the percentage increase (or decrease) in size during the life of the project. It illustrates that projects that shrank by 50 percent or more had lower outcome ratings than projects completed at the planned size; projects that grew by 50 percent or more did about as well as projects with no change in size.[28]

IEG's recent report on additional financing in transport projects (IEG 2015b) found that projects with additional financing had relatively better overall outcome ratings compared with the rest of the portfolio. The analysis also found that providing more resources is no guarantee of success— 13 percent of projects receiving additional resources were rated moderately unsatisfactory or below

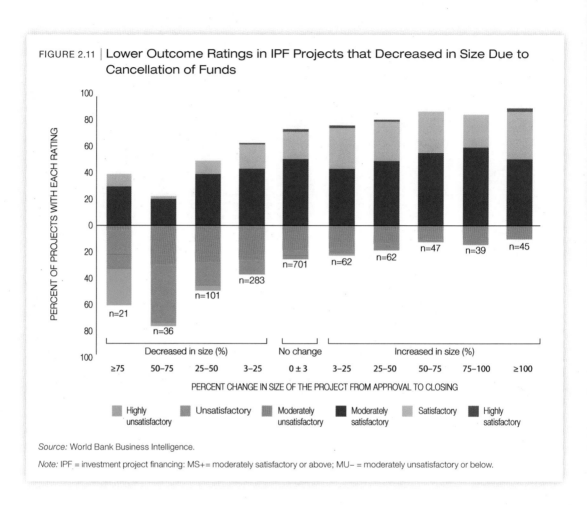

FIGURE 2.11 | Lower Outcome Ratings in IPF Projects that Decreased in Size Due to Cancellation of Funds

PERCENT CHANGE IN SIZE OF THE PROJECT FROM APPROVAL TO CLOSING

Highly unsatisfactory | Unsatisfactory | Moderately unsatisfactory | Moderately satisfactory | Satisfactory | Highly satisfactory

Source: World Bank Business Intelligence.

Note: IPF = investment project financing: MS+ = moderately satisfactory or above; MU– = moderately unsatisfactory or below.

for overall outcomes at project closure. The report, however, notes that a large number of projects received additional financing to cover cost overruns. Therefore, it is highly important to ensure good quality at entry by focusing on preparing realistic engineering designs to avoid substantial cost overruns in the first place. It may be worth noting that additional financing allows Bank project teams to refine the project results framework.

Two other project factors correlated negatively with outcome: the number of task team leaders during the life of the project, and whether the project was ever labeled as problem project.

Projects in the analysis group averaged 2.8 team leaders across the life of the project. Projects did not differ discernibly across regions, but the seven projects in the Trade and Competitiveness GP averaged 4.86 team leaders, while the Social Protection GP averaged 2.47 team leaders per project. Overall, more than half of the projects in the analysis were labeled as problem projects at some point. There was so much variation within GPs that comparison of the different GPs is not informative, but some difference was discernible across regions. The percentage of projects that at some point were labeled as problem projects was 67 percent in the Middle East and North Africa Region, on the high end, and 45 percent in the East Asia and Pacific Region, on the low end (see appendix C for more details on Regions and GPs).

The strong correlation between high team leader turnover and low project outcome is better understood when considering a review of highly satisfactory and unsatisfactory projects conducted for IEG's evaluation of learning and results in World Bank operations (IEG 2015a). The review found that because so much operational and technical knowledge is in the minds of practitioners and is not documented, the gaps in handover between project team leaders is an important source of learning discontinuity. Several team leaders interviewed for the study said there is little overlap of leaders at the time of handover. Handover missions are not conducted systematically, and it is left to team leaders to make time to find staff who worked earlier on in the operation.

In the regression, supervision cost negatively correlated with project outcome ratings, which may indicate that projects experiencing implementation challenges receive greater supervision attention. Supervision costs tended to be higher in the South Asia Region (averaging $910,000) and Africa Region (averaging $867,000), and lower in East Asia and Pacific (averaging $608,000). Preparation cost was not significant for the regression, but East Asia and Pacific had a relatively high average preparation cost ($434,000 per project), while Latin America and the Caribbean had the lowest average preparation cost at $282,000 per project. Box 2.3 draws comparisons with the findings of other research, and appendix C gives further details.

The finding that projects that were ever designated problem projects perform worse than those that were never so designated suggests that early and candid assessment of project implementation performance is important. In-depth portfolio analysis also found that projects that were not restructured in a timely manner were rated moderately unsatisfactory or below. IEG's learning evaluation (2015a) found that the information entered into the World Bank's Implementation Status and Results report is not candid enough, and therefore restructuring does not always take place when it should. This evaluation found no trend to restructure earlier during the project cycle even after introducing the split ratings. In the pre-reform period, the average span between effectiveness and completion was 7.8 years, and the average period between effectiveness and PDO revision was four years. For the post-reform period, the numbers were 7.5 years and 4.4 years, respectively. This suggests that although the split rating rewards early restructuring, introduction of the policy may not have changed the behavior of task team leaders.

To offer a different perspective and an element of triangulation, two analyses of opportunistic data provided examples of project implementation factors associated with outcome ratings. The first analysis (which comes with a caveat because it is based on a particularly small convenience sample of projects) looked at projects reviewed at the Regional Operations Committee or Operations Committee[29] and found higher project ratings for projects that received greater management attention.[30] A second analysis found higher quality at entry in projects that reported baseline data early on.[31]

Box 2.3 | Findings from the Regression Are Consistent with Related Working Papers and Literature

Denizer, Kaufmann, and Kraay (2011) examined country factors and found that the Country Policy and Institutional Assessment, a measure of a country's strength in relation to policies and institutional capacity, correlated with outcome. However, within-country variation pointed to the need to focus on project-level factors such as project size, task manager quality, and early warning signs such as whether the project was labeled as a problem project early on. They also found no evidence that disbursement delays correlated with outcomes.

Geli, Kraay, and Nobakht (2014) analyzed a project's outcomes data to identify project characteristics that might be used to predict project outcomes; they found that Country Policy and Institutional Assessment (CPIA) and the task team leaders' track record had greater predictive power than Implementation Status and Results report ratings, and that initial project size did not correlate with outcomes.

RAP 2014 (IEG 2014b) used text analysis of quality at entry and quality of supervision sections of 203 field-based project assessments completed between FY08 and FY13; the analysis found that elements associated with higher outcome ratings were application of past lessons, effective risk mitigation, and well-articulated project objectives and results frameworks. This analysis also highlighted that World Bank team problem-solving abilities, regularity of missions, and attention to corrective actions were frequently mentioned when explaining the positive quality of supervision ratings.

Quality at entry and project supervision are key to project outcomes

Building on analysis undertaken in RAP 2014 (IEG 2014b), IEG conducted an in-depth portfolio review to identify key factors associated with project outcomes.[32]

The review found that poor quality at entry was a key factor associated with poor outcomes; however, there were no significant differences between small and large projects. Poor quality at entry was associated with the following weaknesses:

- Overambitious or complex project design in the context of insufficient implementing agency capacity (59 percent);

- Poor M&E and results framework (52 percent);

- Unrealistic cost estimation, lessons not incorporated, inadequate safeguards identification, and other design problems (48 percent); and

- Inadequate risk identification and mitigation measures (39 percent).

A number of design issues were identified. For example, about 60 percent of projects had inappropriate indicators, 28 percent lacked baseline data or targets, and 32 percent reported institutional capacity insufficient to operationalize the M&E system.

The IEG electricity access evaluation found that the most important factors for implementation delays were borrower institutional capacity and the World Bank's quality at entry, followed by the government's commitment to the project, and areas of shared responsibility (mainly procurement matters). Shortcomings in institutional capacity affected low- and medium-access countries more than they affected high- and universal-access countries (42 percent versus 10 percent). Quality at entry contributed more often to implementation delays in low- and medium-access countries than in high- and universal-access countries (35 percent versus 19 percent). By contrast, no significant shortcomings were observed in institutional capacity for projects that closed on time, and the World Bank's quality at entry was inadequate in only one of 30 projects (IEG 2015c).

Quality of M&E is also an important finding from the forthcoming IEG report on self-evaluation systems. This analysis finds that M&E has a role beyond "mere measurement of results," because M&E quality is a "strong determinant of satisfactory project ratings." In particular, the analysis found a "rather large and significant effect of quality of monitoring and evaluation on project outcome, accounting for an increase of between 0.13 and 0.40 points in the outcome rating."[33] The study suggests there may be a tipping point—that is, a minimum level of M&E quality needed to make a difference in project ratings because the relationship between M&E quality and project outcomes is not proportional. The findings suggest that improving the quality of M&E in World Bank projects can help the organization achieve targets for project outcome ratings.

Weak project management was a key factor influencing low quality of supervision ratings in the portfolio analysis, including weak fiduciary management, low safeguards compliance, inadequate attention to technical issues and M&E, and so on (Figure 2.12). The analysis found that project teams in these cases were not proactive in revising PDOs or restructuring the project. Untimely support provided by the Bank team to the implementing agency during project implementation relates to weak project management. This can include lack of timely implementation, inadequate and untimely advice to the client, delays in processing documents, and lack of timely follow-up on issues.

The portfolio review also found that Implementation Status and Results (ISR) ratings were not candid; they were overly optimistic and failed to reflect the severity of the problems, and possibly delayed a more proactive response by the World Bank. Analysis undertaken for IEG's learning evaluation found the proportion of projects with below-the-line ratings during implementation was lower than the proportion of projects for which objectives were formally revised, suggesting a lack of candor in ISR ratings—the supervision record understates the number of projects in need of fixing (IEG 2015a).

In poorly supervised projects, task team issues such as expertise, frequent changes in team leadership, untimely succession, and coordination issues within the World Bank team were raised. This is consistent with Geli, Kray, and Nobakht (2014), who found that the record of the team leader significantly correlated with project outcome.

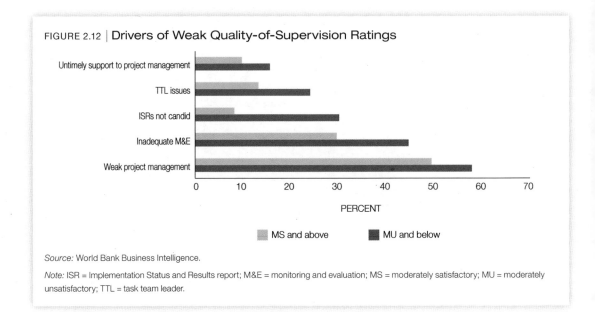

FIGURE 2.12 | Drivers of Weak Quality-of-Supervision Ratings

PERCENT

MS and above   MU and below

Source: World Bank Business Intelligence.

Note: ISR = Implementation Status and Results report; M&E = monitoring and evaluation; MS = moderately satisfactory; MU = moderately unsatisfactory; TTL = task team leader.

For IFC projects, size is not the dominant risk factor

As with Bank projects, IFC investment project success depends on a mix of project characteristics. Overall, IFC investment project performance is better when measured by commitments instead of number of projects. Large projects perform better than small projects, sometimes much better— Figure 2.13 compares the performance of large and small projects.

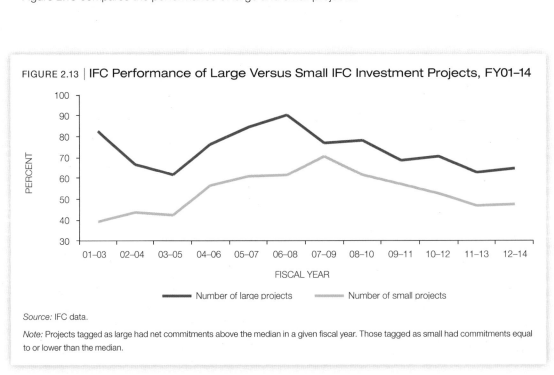

FIGURE 2.13 | IFC Performance of Large Versus Small IFC Investment Projects, FY01–14

PERCENT

FISCAL YEAR

Number of large projects   Number of small projects

Source: IFC data.

Note: Projects tagged as large had net commitments above the median in a given fiscal year. Those tagged as small had commitments equal to or lower than the median.

If size were all that mattered, it could make sense for IFC to focus on larger projects. Although many smaller projects are in large countries, a disproportionate share is in IDA and blend countries, and in smaller countries, as measured by gross domestic product and population (Figure 2.14).

IEG built on its FY13 analysis of internal and external risk factors to assess whether IFC's commitment size is a determinant of project development success. Using only IFC commitment size in its regression model (using 2009–14 evaluations), IEG found that size was a significant correlate of development results for real sector projects, but not for banking projects. However, for real sector projects, the association of commitment size with development success lessened when other risk factors were added to the model. For these projects, external project risks (such as management quality, market conditions, investment climate, and internal controllable risk factors) in IFC's work quality were more significantly correlated with development outcomes.

For financial sector projects, commitment size—together with other risk factors—was marginally but positively associated with project performance. A review of evaluation documents for both successful and unsuccessful financial markets projects reveals a number of benefits associated with size, including:

- **Reach:** Larger financial institutions with a larger geographical and client base are better able to pursue business where demand is highest. They may also be better able to target new client types while continuing to survive on their established markets and client bases, building on their name recognition.

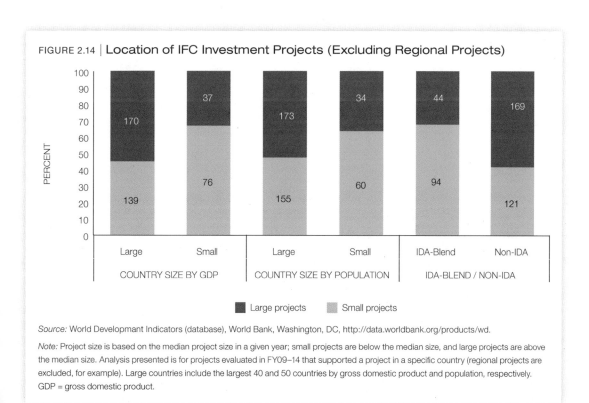

FIGURE 2.14 | Location of IFC Investment Projects (Excluding Regional Projects)

Legend: ■ Large projects ▨ Small projects

Source: World Developmant Indicators (database), World Bank, Washington, DC, http://data.worldbank.org/products/wd.

Note: Project size is based on the median project size in a given year; small projects are below the median size, and large projects are above the median size. Analysis presented is for projects evaluated in FY09–14 that supported a project in a specific country (regional projects are excluded, for example). Large countries include the largest 40 and 50 countries by gross domestic product and population, respectively. GDP = gross domestic product.

- **Economies of scale:** Incremental cost of operations can be lower for larger institutions. They may also be better positioned to deploy superior technology and recruit experts, such as proven managers, environmental specialists, and credit officers.

- **Financial strength:** Larger financial institutions may have a better chance of surviving short-term shocks that affect their business, and may have lower-cost local and international sources of capital.

To summarize, larger IFC commitments to financial sector clients may have some benefits over smaller commitments, but this should not diminish attention to corporate governance, sponsor quality, and IFC work quality, which also drive project success. For real sector projects, internal and external risks drive success more than project size.

Recently committed IFC projects are likely to perform worse than recently evaluated projects, despite a great concentration in lower-risk countries. After identifying the factors associated with development outcomes, IEG analysis predicted how recently committed IFC projects are likely to perform compared with the projects that reached operational maturity and had been evaluated by IEG. Box 2.4 summarizes the results.

Box 2.4 | Performance of Recently Committed IFC Projects Compared with Recently Evaluated Projects

IEG evaluates IFC investment projects at early operating maturity based on their performance to date and projections. Projects that have not reached early operating maturity can be assessed on external risk factors that strongly influence their success, including changes in country risk, management quality, market conditions (real sector projects), corporate governance quality (financial and bank sector projects), and IFC work quality. IEG tested its model with historical data and found that it provides a directionally accurate assessment of development outcomes for projects that have not reached early operating maturity.

IEG found that the external risk for younger real sector projects is slightly higher than for mature, evaluated projects, and the overall risks of younger banking projects is slightly lower (Figure 2.15). Management risk is moving lower for banking projects, but higher for real sector projects. Profit margin risk for real sector projects is higher. Corporate governance risk ratings for banking projects are lower. Country risk, measured by the change in the Institutional Investor Country Credit Risk rating, steadily improved so far. IFC's work quality, a strong mitigant of external risks, steadily declined. IFC's move to lower-risk banking sector projects may downwardly affect its additionality.

IEG's analysis showed that without significant improvements in IFC work quality, development outcomes are likely to decline moderately in 2015 and 2016 (Table 2.1). The greatest risks to development outcomes are profit margin risks for real sector projects. IEG also found that high-quality work could mitigate external risks—that is, activities within IFC's control can increase the chances that a project will succeed. The quality of appraisal had the greatest impact.

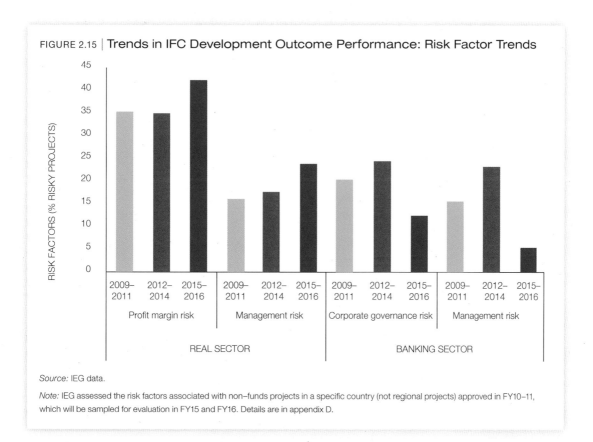

FIGURE 2.15 | Trends in IFC Development Outcome Performance: Risk Factor Trends

Source: IEG data.

Note: IEG assessed the risk factors associated with non–funds projects in a specific country (not regional projects) approved in FY10–11, which will be sampled for evaluation in FY15 and FY16. Details are in appendix D.

TABLE 2.1 | Trends in IFC Development Outcome Performance: Portfolio Performance Calculations

Year	Gap between calculated success rates and actual (Percent)		
2009	0.3		
2010	−2.0		
2011	7.7		
2012	−1.8		
2013	2.7		
2014	1.5		
Success rates for projects to be evaluated in 2015/16 relative to 2012–14 (Percent)			
Year	Real sector	Banking sector	Overall
2015	−1.3	−1.2	−1.2
2016	−3.6	0.1	−2.3

Source: IEG data.

Results and Performance of the World Bank Group at Country Level

World Bank Group country program outcomes continue to improve. Figure 2.16 indicates that on a three-year rolling average basis, the success rate, measured as a percentage of country program outcomes rated as MS or higher, improved from 63 percent in FY12–14 (n=60) to 69 percent in FY13–15 (n=52). This continues an upward trend, from a low of 49 percent in FY10–12 to near the corporate target of 70 percent. Country program outcomes improved in both IBRD and IDA countries. IBRD country program ratings increased from a 78 percent success rate in FY12–14 (n=26) to an 87 percent success rate in FY13–15 (n=23). Country program outcomes in IDA also improved from a 52 percent success rate in FY12–14 (n=33) to a 54 percent success rate in FY13–15 (n=28). For fragile and conflict-affected situation (FCS) countries, program outcomes deteriorated from 80 percent (n=5) in FY12–14 to 75 percent in FY13–15 (n=4).

On an individual year basis, the success rate of country program outcomes improved during the past three fiscal years from 53 percent in FY13 (n=19) to 83 percent in FY15 (n=12), surpassing the Corporate Scorecard target of 70 percent. Among institutions, IBRD's success rate improved from 83 percent in FY13 (n=6) to 88 percent in FY15 (n=8). In the same period, IDA improved from 38 percent (n=13) to 67 percent (n=3). The success rate for fragile and conflict-affected situation country programs was 67 percent in FY13 (n=3). None of the Completion and Learning Reviews for these countries went to the Board in FY15.

The improved performance of World Bank country programs in FY13–15 is driven by Europe and Central Asia and Latin America and the Caribbean (Figure 2.17). For the period FY13–15, the Bank-wide success rate was 69 percent (n=52), up from 63 percent in the period FY12–14 (n=60).[34] The success rates for country programs in Europe and Central Asia and Latin America and the Caribbean improved significantly to 91 percent (n=11 respectively).[35] These performances are much above the World Bank Group average

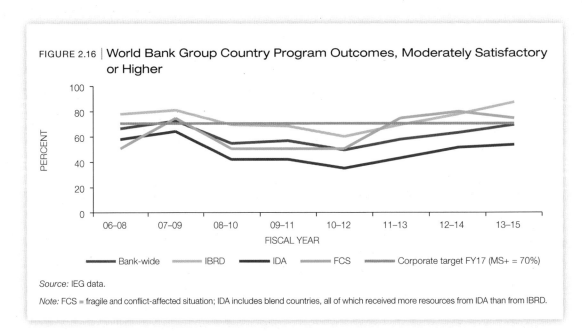

FIGURE 2.16 | World Bank Group Country Program Outcomes, Moderately Satisfactory or Higher

Source: IEG data.

Note: FCS = fragile and conflict-affected situation; IDA includes blend countries, all of which received more resources from IDA than from IBRD.

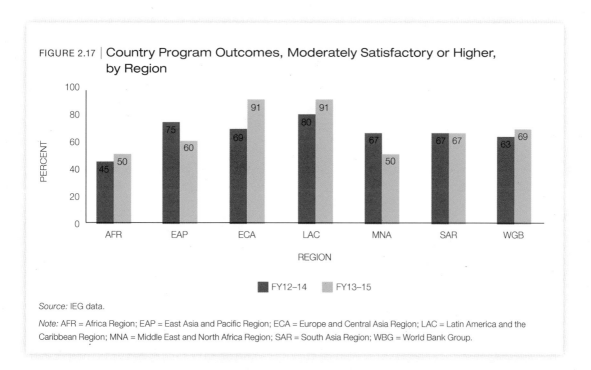

FIGURE 2.17 | Country Program Outcomes, Moderately Satisfactory or Higher, by Region

Source: IEG data.

Note: AFR = Africa Region; EAP = East Asia and Pacific Region; ECA = Europe and Central Asia Region; LAC = Latin America and the Caribbean Region; MNA = Middle East and North Africa Region; SAR = South Asia Region; WBG = World Bank Group.

and the 70 percent corporate target. The success rates for country programs in the Africa Region improved to 50 percent (n=20) in the period FY13–15 while it deteriorated for country programs in the Middle East and North Africa to 50 percent (n=2). The performance of country programs in South Asia remained stable at 67 percent (n=3) or just below the corporate target. Finally, performance of country programs in the East Asia and Pacific Region deteriorated to 60 percent (n=5), below the Bank-wide average and corporate target. It should be noted that even considering a three-year average, the numbers of country programs by Region for which a Completion and Learning Review was submitted to the board are small. In addition, in FY15 there was no Completion and Learning Review submitted to the Board by the East Asia and Pacific Region and the Middle East and North Africa Region.

World Bank Group performance deteriorated slightly (Figure 2.18) between FY12 and FY14 (75 percent, n=60) and between FY13 and FY15 (71 percent, n=52), which is below the corporate target of 75 percent. Performance in IBRD countries improved on a three-year rolling average basis from a 77 percent success rate in FY12–14 (n=26) to a 90 percent success rate in FY13–15 (n=23). Performance in IDA and FCS countries deteriorated from 61 percent (n=33) and 80 percent (n=5) respectively in FY12–14 to 57 percent (n=28) and 75 (n=4) percent in FY13–15.

On a regional basis, the overall slight deterioration of World Bank Group performance for country strategies in the period FY13–15 was driven by the stark deterioration in Latin America and the Caribbean[36] (Figure 2.19). It improved in all other regions, including Africa, or remained stable. In the same period, World Bank Group performance remained below the 75 percent corporate target for the Africa Region (70 percent, n=20), Latin America and the Caribbean (55 percent, n=11) and South Asia (67 percent, n=3).

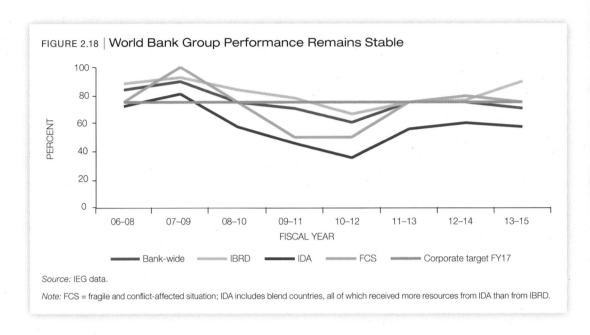

FIGURE 2.18 | World Bank Group Performance Remains Stable

Source: IEG data.

Note: FCS = fragile and conflict-affected situation; IDA includes blend countries, all of which received more resources from IDA than from IBRD.

Closer World Bank–IFC cooperation has the potential to maximize World Bank Group development impact. The World Bank Group's client needs have been changing. The private sector is increasingly becoming the engine of growth, and government attention is shifting from public sector projects to public policies designed to promote private sector–led growth, including regulations, and establishing partnerships with, and/or transferring certain economic activities. This is happening in the context of a growing gap between decreasing official development assistance and growing

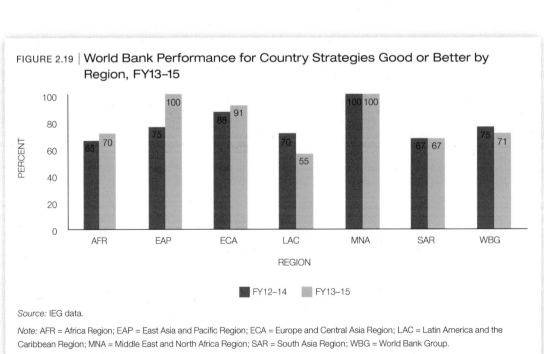

FIGURE 2.19 | World Bank Performance for Country Strategies Good or Better by Region, FY13–15

Source: IEG data.

Note: AFR = Africa Region; EAP = East Asia and Pacific Region; ECA = Europe and Central Asia Region; LAC = Latin America and the Caribbean Region; MNA = Middle East and North Africa Region; SAR = South Asia Region; WBG = World Bank Group.

need for development finance. Private sector investment in development is most needed. In this new landscape, the best way to maximize the World Bank Group's development impact is to foster full use of its private sector instruments and maximize synergies between the World Bank and IFC at the country level.

A recent IEG review, *Past and Future: Bank–IFC Cooperation at the Country Strategy Level*, found that despite some encouraging examples, coordination between the World Bank and IFC at the country strategy level has been mixed, and synergies within the World Bank Group do not seem to have been explored systematically (IEG 2014a).[38]

Five key findings emerged from the review:

- Despite the increase in the number of joint Country Assistance Strategies (CASs), the extent of cooperation between the World Bank and IFC varied significantly across countries, with the majority of country strategies failing to include specific implementation plans for World Bank Group cooperation. References to cooperation, most often, were perfunctory and absent in related results frameworks. This was identified through Country Assistance Strategy Completion Report Reviews.

- Structural constraints exist for the low levels of cooperation at the country strategy level: Market demand determines IFC's business, which inherently makes planning difficult; conflicts of interest are a concern; IFC's strategist and economist resources are extremely limited; and staff incentives may need tailoring to encourage and support cooperation.

- Selective World Bank–IFC cooperation can potentially improve the effectiveness and efficiency of World Bank Group operations and improve its development impact in client countries. However, lack of cooperation can hinder or reduce potential benefits to clients, lead to duplication of activities, and ultimately raise operating costs.

- Genuinely joint Country Assistance Strategy teams led to better coordination and helped clarify the respective roles of the two institutions. Professional relationships between World Bank and IFC staff facilitated knowledge exchange and readiness to work together; however, this cooperation was ad hoc under the Country Assistance Strategy framework.

- Cooperation between the World Bank and IFC is not always necessary or productive for every sector in a country. It should remain an instrument. Elevating it to a goal in itself may generate unnecessary processes and inefficiency. The benefits of cooperation depend on the sector and the stage of its development in a country. The cost of cooperation may sometimes outweigh the benefits, warranting careful cost-benefit analysis at the early stage of new World Bank Group country strategy formation.

Through the new Systematic Country Diagnostics and Country Partnership Framework, the Bank and IFC expect to work more closely together, from diagnosis to strategy formulation, solutions design, execution, evaluation, and learning at the country level. Systematic Country Diagnostics offers the potential to build upon the current Country Assistance Strategy process by increasing World Bank–IFC dialogue and information sharing at the initial stage of the Country Partnership Framework. It could also pave the way for a more systematic analysis of private sector development issues by joint teams, which has historically been missing from the majority of CASs. This process may provide a consistent framework to define and enable potential synergies generated by the cooperation in relevant, selective areas of engagement.

The review (IEG 2014a) identified a number of factors that help drive cooperation between the World Bank and IFC, including:

- Good, professional working relationships and knowledge sharing between World Bank and IFC staff (in Kenya, Rwanda, and Uganda).

- Strong government leadership or ownership (in China, Egypt, and Russia) for Bank–IFC cooperation

- Senior management commitment to facilitating cooperation and/or well-developed working relationships between senior Bank and IFC managements (in East Asia and Pacific Region)

- Close communication (and co-location, where business conditions permit) between World Bank and IFC country offices (in Egypt).[39]

To realize the potential of World Bank–IFC cooperation, both the Bank and IFC need to provide explicit incentives. Under the new country engagement model, staff and manager performance reviews may include references to cooperation across World Bank Group institutions. This would provide incentives to the institutions' staff to learn and understand the methods of operation, strengths, and limitations of the other institution, and may eventually lead to effective cooperation. Another option is to encourage staff rotations between the Bank and IFC so that more World Bank Group staff can better understand the World Bank or IFC operations.

Along with effective incentives, appropriate resources should be devoted to cooperation. In particular, full participation by IFC in the Country Partnership Framework process would require a significant increase in the number of IFC regional strategists and economists. Providing incentives to Bank economists to work on private sector issues can partly alleviate the budget implications, and by incorporating IFC sector economists, results measurement specialists, and the World Bank's sector specialists with private sector knowledge into the new Country Partnership Framework process.

As planned under the new World Bank Group strategy, much progress has been done in implementing new instruments and mechanisms designed to substantially strengthen intra-agency cooperation both at the design and implementation levels. Guidelines for producing Systematic Country Diagnostics and Country Partnership Frameworks have been issued in CY14, and by end of December 2015, diagnostics and frameworks for 17 countries have been submitted to the Board. In addition, the World Bank Group has set up Joint Implementation Plans and Regional Coordination Mechanism and is expected to increase the number of joint projects.

Through reviews of Completion and Learning Reviews, IEG will continue to evaluate the new World Bank Group country engagement model under the Country Partnership Framework to assess whether it is leading to improved cooperation and better development results at the country level. In addition, the ongoing process evaluation of Systematic Country Diagnostics and Country Partnership Frameworks, a real-time evaluation will provide evaluative input into the operationalization and rollout of the World Bank Group's new country engagement approach. Furthermore, IEG will evaluate joint implementation plans while they formally become part of the new Country Partnership Framework process to determine whether these management tools contribute to more effective cooperation at the country level. IEG is preparing a Learning Note on lessons from World Bank Group experience with joint projects, to be delivered end-FY16.

ENDNOTES

[1] The $60 billion includes IBRD and IDA lending, IFC long-term financing, MIGA guarantees, and Recipient-Executed Trust Funds commitments of $3.9 billion. Reflecting current practice (World Bank Group Annual Report 2015), short-term finance or funds mobilized from other investors are not included in the calculation of overall commitments, as they were in the RAP 2014 (IEG 2014b).

[2] Any effects of the shift from the old sectors to Global Practices on project performance would not be expected to show up until three to seven years in the future, because performance is assessed after projects close. Project Completion Reports are normally due six months after project closure, and IEG validation occurs only after that. This report covers commitment data through FY15, and performance data on projects closed in FY14 and earlier that have IEG-validated ratings.

[3] IFC changed its reporting practices regarding short-term investment amounts beginning in FY15. The change better aligns IFC with the approach used by commercial banks, but it also makes it difficult to compare IFC's FY15 commitment volume with that of previous years. IFC now reports its average outstanding short-term finance balance instead of total commitments. IEG welcomes the change.

[4] MIGA offers two kinds of guarantees in this category: Non-Honoring of a Sovereign Financial Obligation, and Non-Honoring of Financial Obligation by a State-Owned Enterprise. These guarantees do not require a final arbitral award or court decision as a condition for paying a claim. See http://www.miga.org/investment-guarantees for a description of MIGA's guarantee products.

[5] The cutoff date for the World Bank portfolio performance data used in this report is November 25, 2015.

[6] Net commitment is the final size of the project in U.S. dollars. If some project funds were canceled during implementation, the net commitment is smaller than the initial commitment, which is the size of the project at approval. If funds were added through additional financing, the net commitment is larger than the initial commitment.

[7] In this report, as in its predecessors, success rate is defined as the share of projects whose outcome rating is moderately satisfactory, satisfactory, or highly satisfactory on a six-point scale used by IEG for Implementation Completion and Results (ICR) reviews.

[8] As noted in Moll, Geli, and Saavedra (2015), "Policy-based loans are intended to support a set of policy and institutional reforms in a country. They do not directly finance physical infrastructure and are not earmarked as are investment projects. Policy-based loans are shorter in time span and all prior actions/conditions are met before the presentation of the loan to the World Bank Board of Executive Directors."

[9] Project efficiency is not rated for development policy financing projects.

[10] Because IEG has not yet validated any Program for Results projects as of October 2015, this instrument is not included in Figure 2.2.

[11] The IBRD classification for World Bank projects is based on the type of agreement when the project is approved.

[12] Examples of clear-cut and straightforward project development objectives (PDOs) included access to services or enhancement of environmental services. Examples of multifaceted and long-duration PDOs included crop diversification, increased productivity, and associated welfare outcomes.

[13] IEG rated six IBRD, 11 IDA, and 32 Global Environment Facility projects in FY12–14.

[14] It is important to note significant variation in the number and type of projects in respective practices. The largest number of projects rated for a single Global Practice (GP) during FY12–14 is 53 for the Macroeconomics and Fiscal Management GP, compared with 11 for the Governance GP, and nine for the Finance and Markets GP.

[15] IEG validated 226 IFC investment projects in FY12–14. One of these projects could not be rated for development outcome. Accordingly, many of the tables in the document refer to 225 projects.

[16] IFC projects are selected for evaluation based on a stratified, random, statistically representative sample of net approved projects for each calendar year, including closed projects.

[17] See http://ieg.worldbankgroup.org/methodology for more details on IFC's rating methodology.

[18] More information on IFC's self-evaluation systems, including the quality of self-evaluation and lessons, are in IEG's forthcoming evaluation of the World Bank Group's self-evaluation systems.

[19] About 37 percent of the financial markets projects evaluated are rated category C and are expected to have minimal or no adverse environmental or social impacts. Category C projects are not rated for environmental and social effects. Of the projects that were categorized FI (investments that themselves have no adverse social or environmental impacts, but may finance subprojects with potential impacts), 67 percent were rated less than satisfactory for ESH or could not be rated because of insufficient information, and 20 percent were rated satisfactory or above. IEG did not rate the remaining projects because they had minimal or no adverse impacts.

[20] A separate model for performance of IFC projects exists, developed over several years. Investment success is a key aspect of IFC project performance, and it is not applicable to World Bank projects. This analysis focuses on World Bank investment lending projects.

[21] Previous RAP reports included information on the difference (or "disconnect") between IEG's validation ratings and the self-evaluation ratings in ICRs. In the recent period, the disconnect narrowed for both World Bank and IFC projects, though less so for DPFs. The forthcoming IEG report on self-evaluation systems found that the strong focus on ratings and the disconnect with IEG are a distraction from learning. This report omits the discussion of disconnect to focus on elements that offer more insight and potential for learning.

[22] Consistent with previous RAP reports, this analysis excludes DPFs, which are fewer in number and larger in commitment size than investment project financing (IPF) projects. The method for arriving at outcome ratings also differs. Analysis by Operations Policy and Country Services found no significant difference in project size between DPFs and IPFs (Moll, Geli, and Saavedra 2015).

[23] Among the IPF projects closed in FY09–14, the correlation coefficients with outcome rating were 0.67 for quality at entry, 0.66 for quality of supervision, and 0.54 for monitoring and evaluation (M&E) quality. In comparison, the correlation coefficients were 0.13 for initial commitment (log), 0.24 for net commitment (log), and 0.37 for the change in size between initial and net commitment (log).

[24] The Corporate Scorecard and other internal documents measure volume, or lending volume, by the size of net commitment (the difference between initial commitment and final project size). In the past decade, the volume-weighted percentage of successful projects was consistently higher than the unweighted percentage of successful projects (Figure 2.2). This observation indicates some relationship between project size and project outcome ratings; however, both project size and project ratings also correlated with other factors related to country context and project implementation.

[25] IEG developed the regression model for IBRD and IDA–funded Investment Project Financing (IPF) that closed during FY09–14. The analysis focuses on IPFs only because the evaluation methodology is different for DPFs and IPFs. IEG excluded grants because of inadequate data.

Data used in the ordered logistic regression included project outcome rating, initial commitment amount, and change in commitment amount between approval and closing. Appendix B lists additional variables used to assess their correlations with project outcome ratings.

The regression analysis was conducted with the caveat that the variables available probably do not capture performance during supervision, and especially midcourse correction. IEG relies on ex-post ratings of project quality, and an important limitation is the lack of a systematic assessment of quality at entry at project approval.

[26] The main regression analysis used Country Policy and Institutional Assessment (CPIA) as a measure of country context, but the Gender Inequality Index for the country would have been significant if substituted for CPIA in the model. The same would be true for World Governance Indicators for Government Effectiveness and Rule of Law. However, these indicators are highly correlated with CPIA, so the model used only CPIA. Operational strategies and the developmental mandate of World Bank Group institutions ensure that operations are undertaken in eligible countries based on multiple criteria.

[27] Of the IBRD- and IDA-funded IPF projects included in the regression analysis, 64 percent had lower net commitment than initial commitment (some funds were canceled or not disbursed). Twelve percent of projects had no cancellations or additions. Twenty-four percent of projects had higher net commitment than initial commitment (they had additional financing).

[28] Larger cancellation was associated with lower performance ratings when the regression model was run with only projects that had cancellations. Running the regression for only projects that had either no change or additional financing, the coefficient for the difference in project size was positive but no longer significant.

[29] Most projects conduct a formal review of the Project Appraisal Document (PAD) at a meeting chaired by the Country Director. However, certain high-risk projects are discussed at the Regional Operations Committee (chaired by the Regional Vice-President) or at the Operations Committee, in which case the project often receives additional attention during preparation for these meetings. It may also receive additional attention during implementation.

[30] Between FY08 and FY13, the Regional Operations Committee reviewed 163 projects under preparation, and the Operations Committee reviewed 26 projects. (Data were based on an Operations Policy and Country Services (OPCS) list of projects reviewed at the Regional Operations Committee or the Operations Committee during FY08–13.) Of these 189 projects, 22 closed by FY14 and had Implementation Completion and Results Review (ICRR) ratings. Nineteen of these 22 projects had ICRR ratings for overall project outcome, and 17 of the 19 (89 percent) were rated moderately satisfactory or above. In comparison, among the 664 IBRD and IDA projects closed in FY09–14 with ICRR ratings, 70 percent were rated moderately satisfactory or above. This difference was statistically significant at the 90 percent confidence level ($p < 0.1$). The Z score was 1.79. At the more commonly used 95 percent confidence level ($p < 0.05$), this difference was not significant.

[31] This analysis used a convenience sample of data produced by the Operations Policy and Country Services (OPCS) review of first Implementation Status and Results (ISRs) for IDA projects, and found that in projects where baseline data were available for PDO indicators at the time of the first ISR, quality at entry ratings were higher than in projects where baseline data were available for only some indicators at the time of the first ISR. For reporting in the Corporate Scorecard, OPCS reviews the first ISRs produced for IDA projects. The review records the number of PDO indicators listed, and whether the ISR reports baseline data for all, some, or none of the indicators. The analysis is used on 346 IDA projects reviewed during FY07–14 that closed and had ICRR ratings. Among the projects in which the first ISR contained baseline data for all PDO indicators, 73 percent (155 out of 212) had quality at entry ratings of moderately satisfactory or above in the ICRR compared with 60 percent (49 out of 81) for projects that had baseline data for only some PDO indicators at first ISR. This difference was statistically significant.

[32] This analysis was used on a random sample drawn from investment projects that closed during FY12–14. The sample was at 90 percent confidence level. Moderately unsatisfactory projects were stratified by small and large (83 projects were selected), and 61 moderately satisfactory projects were selected. Small projects were those with net commitment of $25 million or less, and large projects had net commitment of more than $25 million.

[33] This increase is associated with a one-point increase in the M&E quality rating, using two types of project outcome ratings (from self-evaluation and from IEG validation). Note that the M&E quality rating is on a four-point scale, and the project outcome rating is on a six-point scale.

[34] For calculating the country program success rate, IEG considered only Completion and Learning Reviews with a country program rating.

[35] None of these success rates are statically significant at conventional levels.

[36] In FY15, seven of the 12 Completion and Learning Reviews submitted to the Board were for countries in the Latin America and the Caribbean region, and World Bank Performance was rated fair or below for five of those: Argentina, Costa-Rica, Dominican Republic, Panama, and Paraguay.

[37] IEG reviewed Country Assistance Strategy Completion Report reviews completed during FY12–14 and other relevant work, including the IEG 2010 *Evaluation Brief, World Bank Group Cooperation: Evidence and Lessons from IEG Valuation,* the IDA–IFC Secretariat's 2009 *Models of Joint Strategy Formulation* and IEG's 2007 *IFC Cooperation with the World Bank in the Middle Income Countries, 1996–2006.*

[38] The significance of communications between Bank and IFC country offices recently became crucial since both the Bank and IFC succeeded in decentralizing their operations to regional hubs and countries. Consistent communications between the Bank and IFC, though seemingly elemental, is an important contributor to better understanding and cooperation between the two institutions at the country level.

REFERENCES

Denizer, Cevdet, Daniel Kaufmann, and Aart Kraay. 2013. "Good Countries or Good Projects? Macro and Micro Correlates of World Bank Project Performance." Journal of Development Economics 105 (November): 288–302.

Geli, Patricia, Aart C. Kraay, and Hoveida Nobakht. 2014. "Predicting World Bank Project Outcome Ratings." Policy Research Working Paper No. 7001, World Bank, Washington, DC.

Independent Evaluation Group (IEG). 2011. *Social Safety Nets: An Evaluation of World Bank Support, 2000–2010.* Washington, DC: World Bank.

———. 2014a. *Past and Future: Bank–IFC Cooperation at the Country Strategy Level.* Washington, DC: World Bank.

———. 2014b. *Results and Performance of the World Bank Group 2014.* Washington, DC: World Bank.

———. 2015a. *Learning and Results in World Bank Operations: Toward a New Learning Strategy (Evaluation 2).* Washington, DC: World Bank.

———. 2015b. *Learning Note: Additional Financing for Transport and Information and Communication Technology (ICT).* Washington, DC: World Bank.

International Finance Corporation (IFC). 2015. *Management's Discussion and Analysis and Condensed Consolidated Financial Statements September 30, 2015.* Washington, DC: IFC.

Moll, Peter, Patricia Geli, and Pablo Saavedra. 2015. "Correlates of Success in World Bank Development Policy Lending." Policy Research Working Paper No. 7181, World Bank, Washington, DC.

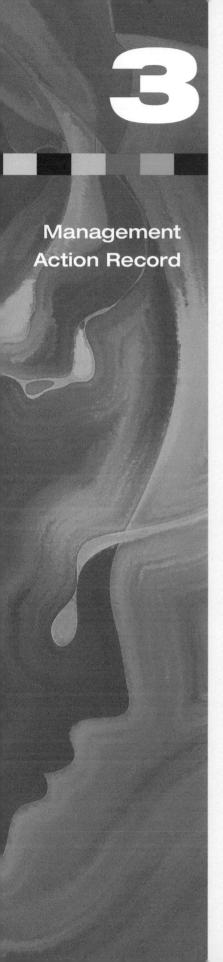

3

Management Action Record

highlights

1 The Management Action Record (MAR) process has been successful in creating a formal, transparent, and well-understood structure within the organization for reporting about progress being made to address recommendations in IEG evaluations

2 At the end of four years of review, implementation of the vast majority of recommendations (more than 80 percent) are rated substantial or higher

3 An in-depth review of the six evaluations exiting the MAR this year found that evaluations are most influential when they are timely, strategically relevant, and credible, and include early and frequent stakeholder engagement to create ownership

4 For evaluations that address difficult or cross-cutting issues with unclear ownership, early engagement with the right stakeholder may not be achieved. Such evaluations may nevertheless be among the most influential in the longer run

Background

IEG EVALUATIONS are part of a system aimed at improving the development effectiveness of World Bank Group programs and activities and their responsiveness to member countries' needs and concerns. The Management Action Record (MAR) process aims to create transparency about progress made by World Bank Group management in addressing IEG recommendations, which serve to offer focus on specific issues.

Tracking and rating actions to address recommendations is an annual and publicly monitorable process. IEG and World Bank Group management use the MAR process to track actions taken in line with recommendations made by IEG in sector, thematic, and corporate evaluations. Management reports on progress made each year, and both management and IEG independently assess and rate implementation. IEG discloses these assessments and ratings on the IEG website. Box 3.1 describes the MAR process in more detail.

A study of the influence of IEG evaluations (IEG 2011b) and follow-up interviews carried out in 2015 with six evaluations entering their fourth and last year of MAR follow-up show that the timeliness, quality, and relevance of IEG's evaluations affect their influence. IEG's evaluations are most influential when significant engagement and information sharing occurs between IEG and its World Bank Group counterparts throughout the evaluative process, and not just immediately before disclosure.

How well are recommendations implemented?

An evaluation's overall influence is difficult to measure, because influence may not be recognized or acknowledged, may take time, and may affect ways of thinking instead of directly related actions. However, the MAR ratings indicate how well the World Bank Group has implemented actions that are in line with the recommendations. The implementation experience is diverse. By the end of FY15, IEG and the World Bank Group tracked actions for 170 recommendations across the World Bank, IFC, and MIGA, drawn from the 25 evaluations produced between FY11 and FY14. It is difficult to draw major conclusions, given that these 25 evaluations launched within four years, and that the dataset is relatively small and built on a group of highly diverse evaluations. IEG and the Bank tracked only six evaluations for year 1, nine for year 2, four evaluations for year 3, and six evaluations for year 4. The evaluations covered a wide range of topics within sectors (agriculture and agribusiness, forestry, transport, health financing, for example), themes (such as harmonization, innovation, public-private partnerships), and policies and procedures (for example, safeguards and procurement). Drawing conclusions on the overall implementation experience is also difficult because only six of the evaluations were in their last year of implementation tracking.

Box 3.1 | What Is the Management Action Record and How Is It Used?

The Management Action Record is a process to create structured opportunities for IEG and World Bank Group management to follow up on IEG recommendations and management actions related to IEG's corporate, sector, and thematic evaluations. IEG has tracked management's actions in response to its recommendations since the late 1990s for the World Bank, since 2003 for MIGA, and since 2004 for IFC. Management's responses and self-assessment, and IEG's assessment of these responses have been disclosed since 2010.

IEG and World Bank Group management have adhered to the following process since FY13:

- IEG clarifies the link between the evaluation findings and the recommendations, and discusses the recommendations with management before finalizing them.

- Management prepares a plan with actions and timelines after the Board discusses an evaluation.

- IEG offers a final set of comments on the action plan.

- IEG begins tracking the level of implementation of the recommendations (one fiscal year after the Board discussion) based on indicators and targets in the plan, and tracks recommendations for four years. Management updates IEG on actions taken, and rates its implementation progress annually on the following scale: negligible, moderate, substantial, high, and complete. IEG reviews and evaluates each management update and separately rates management's actions on the same scale.

An online system implemented in FY14 streamlines the tracking and updating process and ensures consistency in reporting across the World Bank Group.

Monitoring the actions associated with IEG recommendations generates knowledge on areas where improvements are made and where they are not. It also serves an accountability function by informing the Board's Committee on Development Effectiveness and the public about management's actions in response to evaluation recommendations. The process does not include specific activities to encourage the use of knowledge accumulated throughout the updates.

The World Bank Group made progress on its Action Plans, and its and IEG's assessments of progress align with each other over time. Toward the end of the four years that the World Bank Group gives itself to respond to IEG recommendations, both management and IEG rate implementation of the majority (more than 80 percent) of recommendations substantial or higher (Figure 3.1).

Implementation progress does not vary across the major categories of recommendations except for those related to improving monitoring and evaluation (M&E). IEG recommendations can be categorized as strategy, policy, programs, projects, knowledge development, M&E, or other operational issues. Among the 170 recommendations tracked this year, the largest group (39 percent) covers Strategy and Policy (Figure 3.2). Most of the 25 evaluations analyzed included a recommendation for better M&E deployment, specifically: strengthening results frameworks and indicators to better assess the impact of interventions; working with the client to build capacity to collect data and conduct M&E; or establishing M&E systems for new or cross-cutting areas, such as innovation and entrepreneurship, public-private partnerships, and procurement.

Although management generally agreed with IEG's M&E recommendations, implementation proved difficult. The most frequently cited causes for sluggish implementation were issues with data collection, the methodologies for assessing project impacts and developing outcomes, and the time taken for outcomes to materialize. Management's annual updates acknowledged the difficulties in strengthening M&E; the rating for M&E recommendation implementation was lower than average. In the fourth and last year of follow-up, management rated only two of the four M&E-related recommendations as having substantial or better implementation progress, which is significantly less than the progress ratings for other recommendations.

Implementation progress depends on context. Recent developments within the World Bank Group also affected specific evaluations. For example, the transition to a Global Practice structure in FY15 delayed implementation of actions for the *Improving Institutional Capability and Financial Viability to Sustain Transport* evaluation (IEG 2013). IEG rated actions for three recommendations from the evaluation of IFC's poverty focus (IEG 2011a) low because changes in IFC's focus weakened the impetus of some of the agreed actions and raised questions on the sustainability of some previous actions.

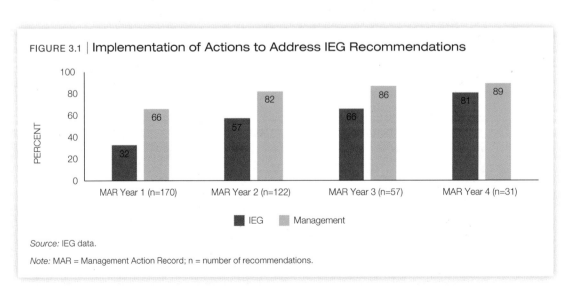

FIGURE 3.1 | **Implementation of Actions to Address IEG Recommendations**

Source: IEG data.

Note: MAR = Management Action Record; n = number of recommendations.

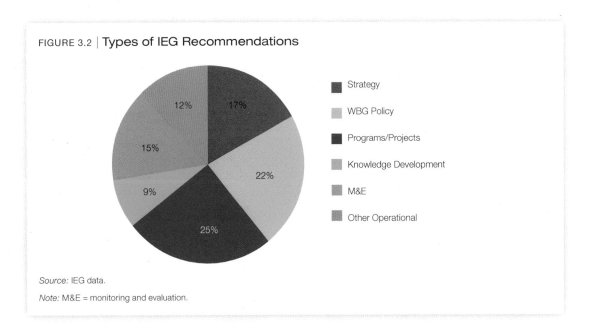

FIGURE 3.2 | Types of IEG Recommendations

- Strategy
- WBG Policy
- Programs/Projects
- Knowledge Development
- M&E
- Other Operational

17%
22%
25%
9%
15%
12%

Source: IEG data.

Note: M&E = monitoring and evaluation.

How well does the MAR work?

IEG undertook more detailed analysis of four years of implementation tracking of six evaluations for a better understanding of the progress made in addressing evaluation findings and recommendations, and the broader experiences the MAR process offered to the various parties involved. The methodology adopted for the in-depth review included a desk review of the evaluations and their corresponding MAR updates, and semi-structured interviews with IEG and World Bank Group managers and staff involved with the evaluations and their MAR updates, using a standardized interview template.

IEG found that management was responsive, but the process itself was too mechanical to have truly supported the evaluations' influence. IEG found that junior staff or consultants frequently prepare the annual management updates, which are usually just a desk-based write-up with reviews that rarely include dialogue between management and IEG and across various involved parties in the World Bank Group. Little deep self-reflection happens among the various stakeholders that would have been involved in actual implementation.

The extent to which World Bank Group management agrees to and buys into recommendations affects the level of World Bank Group engagement during the implementation. For example, in response to the evaluation of the World Bank's trust fund activities (IEG 2011d), the World Bank introduced the Management Framework for World Bank Partnership Programs and Financial Intermediary Funds, addressing the need to strengthen guidance for accepting and managing financial intermediary funds. After the evaluation of social safety nets (IEG 2011c), the World Bank increased lending for social safety net operations, including increases in low-income countries. The increased funding helped to build systems that enhance the ability of countries to cope with shocks; these significant advances were achieved by the final year of follow-up on the original recommendations. It is unclear whether the evaluation can take much credit for this development. It could be that the recommendations were in line with what the sector would have done anyway, which the evaluation further legitimized. Across the board, though, IEG and World Bank Group managers and staff interviewed found the format of the update process bureaucratic and limiting.

It is important to understand the contribution of the MAR process to an evaluation's influence in the context of the evaluation and its specific influence potential. Many factors affect evaluation influence, and a broad and evolving literature identifies three attributes that characterize influential evaluations: timeliness and strategic relevance, analytical quality and credibility, and depth and frequency of building engagement with and ownership by management. Interviews with selected managers and staff involved with the evaluations confirmed these categories, in line with an earlier review of IEG influence, which concluded that a constructive feedback loop between the IEG evaluation team and management could enhance IEG's contribution to World Bank Group development effectiveness.[1] More specifically, the in-depth review found the following:

- **On timeliness and strategic relevance:** Evaluations that were timely and generated findings and recommendations that aligned with ongoing strategic priorities and operational programs tended to have relatively stronger influence. For example, a review of IFC's Performance Standards was underway when IEG completed the evaluation *Safeguards and Sustainability Policies in a Changing World: An Independent Evaluation of World Bank Group Experience* (2010b). According to those interviewed, the IEG evaluation informed the IFC review. The managers and staff interviewed noted that IFC's updated Performance Standards (adopted in 2011) are largely consistent with IEG's recommendations. Timing also mattered if a similar or related evaluation was issued shortly before: Interviewees confirmed that they found one of the evaluations studied to be less influential because another evaluation with similar recommendations was released only a few years earlier.

- **On analytical quality and credibility:** Managers and staff interviewed confirmed that the report's analytical quality and the evaluation team's technical credibility strongly influenced how seriously they took the report and its recommendations. It would be difficult to rate analytical quality or credibility across the six evaluations in a meaningful way, given their topical, contextual, and methodological differences, and the fact that the dataset of six evaluations is too small to draw statistically relevant conclusions about the relationship between quality and influence.

- **On ownership:** Evaluations that created early buy-in to findings and recommendations ultimately had strong management ownership, with implications for actions and their implementation. Management interviewed specifically noted that they were informed about issues associated with the topic and key findings early on and could discuss them. When the evaluation report was finalized, management did not have to deal with surprises and could act swiftly on the recommendations. Those interviewed confirmed that such early engagement allowed them to assume accountability for actions more easily than when they felt forced to do so when confronted with findings and recommendations at the end. The evaluation of social safety nets (IEG 2011c) is, again, a good example: The lead evaluator proactively engaged early with the Sector Board at the time, creating ample space for dialogue on emerging issues and insights. Ownership and early engagement are desirable; however, it is important to note that these may not be achieved for evaluations that address difficult issues in the World Bank Group, or cross-cutting issues with unclear ownership. Such evaluations may still be among the most influential in the longer term, but the influence may take more time, and avenues of influence may be required other than what the MAR can offer. A statement in the Independent Panel's report to the Committee on Development Effectiveness (CODE) stressed the importance of IEG's strategic engagement and a close but uncompromised relationship with management and staff.

How can MAR potential be tapped?

The *External Review of the Independent Evaluation of the World Bank Group Report to CODE from the Independent Panel* (IEG 2015) also suggested the need for stronger initial buy-in on evaluation findings and recommendations. The report stated, "Current weaknesses in the way CODE, IEG, and management interact prevent the World Bank Group from fully benefiting from independent evaluation." Two of the panel's eight recommendations refer to MAR-related processes, and improvements in the MAR process could contribute to addressing several concerns raised by the panel. The panel's statement is notable in this context: "A number of those interviewed stressed that the effectiveness and capacity of an independent evaluation unit to influence and bring about change requires strategic engagement and a close, but uncompromised, relationship with management and staff. IEG's isolation and interpretation of independence has created tense and formalized relationships, too much focus on process, and an overdependence on the quality of human dynamics and interactions."

The shortcomings of the MAR process relate mostly to the lack of dialogue and dynamic engagement. Most managers and staff regarded the MAR follow-up as a static accounting exercise that did not fully consider the dynamic environment within which World Bank Group units operate. They also thought the evaluation and the broader issues and challenges to the World Bank Group it identified were lost because of the limited focus on a set of specific and fixed actions. The move toward actions and timelines further emphasized the mechanical dimension of assessing progress made toward implementation. Consequently, many of those interviewed in both the World Bank Group and IEG perceived the process as having limited value for learning and operational use.

Previous reforms of the MAR process introduced guidelines for writing recommendations, suggested earlier engagement, and stipulated the introduction of Action Plans with indicators and timelines. Having addressed some of the more mechanical aspects of the MAR process, future work will need to focus on ongoing stakeholder and ownership issues.

A new round of improvements to the MAR process should focus on bringing purpose back to the Action Plans and the annual updates, including stocktaking at the final update. A close collaboration among CODE, the Bank, IFC, MIGA, and IEG should design and implement a further round of improvements to the MAR process. Topics to consider are:

- Earlier and more in-depth engagement by the evaluators with management and topical stakeholders

- Expanding the boundaries for updates beyond the specific actions

- Introducing a learning dialogue at the end of the update process.

ENDNOTE

[1] An earlier review of the influence of IEG evaluation on the World Bank Group found that the factors contributing to the increased influence of these evaluations included a sense of shared ownership of the evaluation; credibility of evaluation results; methodological rigor; the coherence, clarity, and cost effectiveness of recommendations; the extent of interaction between evaluators and management; the timeliness of the evaluation; the presence of advocates for reform and adoption of IEG recommendations; and institutional incentives and accountability for adopting recommendations. The review stated that a constructive feedback loop could enhance the effectiveness of the World Bank Group (IEG 2011b).

REFERENCES

Independent Evaluation Group (IEG). 2011a. *Assessing IFC's Poverty Focus and Results.* Washington, DC: World Bank.

———. 2011b. *IEG Annual Report 2011: Results and Performance of the World Bank Group.* Washington, DC: World Bank.

———. 2011c. *Social Safety Nets: An Evaluation of World Bank Support, 2000–2010.* Washington, DC: World Bank.

———. 2011d. *Trust Funds for Development: An Evaluation of the World Bank's Trust Fund Portfolio.* Washington, DC: World Bank.

———. 2013. *Improving Institutional Capability and Financial Viability to Sustain Transport: An Evaluation of World Bank Group Support Since 2002.* Washington, DC: World Bank.

———. 2015. *External Review of the Independent Evaluation of the World Bank Group Report to CODE from the Independent Panel, June 2015.* Washington, DC: World Bank.